I0620142

ERIKA DANIELS, LCSW

Bringing Dad Home

A Practical Guide to Healing the Void Left by an Absent Father

First published by ReUnity Solutions 2022

Copyright © 2022 by Erika Daniels, LCSW

All rights reserved. No part of this publication may be reproduced, stored or transmitted in any form or by any means, electronic, mechanical, photocopying, recording, scanning, or otherwise without written permission from the publisher. It is illegal to copy this book, post it to a website, or distribute it by any other means without permission.

Erika Daniels, LCSW asserts the moral right to be identified as the author of this work.

Erika Daniels, LCSW has no responsibility for the persistence or accuracy of URLs for external or third-party Internet Websites referred to in this publication and does not guarantee that any content on such Websites is, or will remain, accurate or appropriate.

Designations used by companies to distinguish their products are often claimed as trademarks. All brand names and product names used in this book and on its cover are trade names, service marks, trademarks and registered trademarks of their respective owners. The publishers and the book are not associated with any product or vendor mentioned in this book. None of the companies referenced within the book have endorsed the book.

Cover art by Terrance Daniels

First edition

ISBN: 979-8-218-02919-7

This book was professionally typeset on Reedsy.
Find out more at reedsy.com

I dedicate this book to the memory of Robert Parker, my birth father who is the inspiration for this book, and to the memory of William "Andad" Gunn, for being the first father figure in my life. Finally, to Howard Rose, my stepfather—who has been a real father to me since the age of five—for being my main father figure and loving me as if I was your own, and giving me a good life. Thank you all for healing my void.

Contents

Preface

Congratulations on taking the first step in working out your absent father issues. Some individuals are unaware of the effect father absence has on their life. They act as if the pain, thoughts, or feelings do not exist. They suppress and avoid dealing with these painful feelings.

First, let's take a look at the problem. Father absence represents one of the most detrimental social trends of our times. According to the 2020 US Census Bureau, in America, 23.6% of children (18.3 million), or one out of four, lived without a biological, step, or adoptive father in the home. According to the National Fatherhood Initiative, children from father-absent homes are at four times greater risk of poverty, more likely to have behavioral problems, two times greater risk of infant mortality, more likely to go to prison, more likely to commit a crime, seven times more likely to become pregnant, more likely to face child abuse and neglect, more likely to abuse drugs and alcohol, two times more likely to suffer obesity, and two times more likely to drop out of high school. Without going into great detail about these statistics, I believe you can see the point—father absence has severe ramifications.

That is why I felt it was crucial to address this issue in my book and in my career. Father absence has a significant impact on a child's life. It is a social problem and can be considered an epidemic. I believe this is an epidemic because it is a widespread occurrence that's so common and accepted as a part of life in the United States of America. This epidemic has its symptoms and creates a sense of emptiness in one's life (the individual with an absent biological father). In this book, you will learn ways to heal this fatherless void.

Unfortunately, there are many reasons that a father is physically absent.

They may be unavailable due to circumstances that are out of their control. Some fathers would probably want to be involved if they had the opportunity. One needs to understand the circumstances surrounding the father's absence. A father may be absent due to the child's mother not wanting the father to be in the child's life. But this is not a good enough reason to keep a child from their father. If the parents were young when they had the child, then their maturity level can play a role in influencing their decision-making abilities. Also, their parents can influence the decision of the father's involvement.

Other circumstances include not knowing he was the child's father. There are many instances where a man and a woman have a brief relationship, go their separate ways, then the woman realizes she's pregnant but doesn't communicate this with the father. In this case, one can't blame the father because he may have wanted to be involved if he had been aware. The child would never know. How would he ever know to seek his child out unless he has heard about his child and is aware of his child's existence? He is at a disadvantage.

Another reason a father may be absent is if the parents divorce and go their separate ways. Maybe the divorce was conflictual, and the parents ended on bad terms. This situation will impact the father-child relationship since the parents do not want anything to do with each other. Sadly, parents lack understanding of how an absent father affects their child's life. The child becomes collateral damage, as the intention of the divorce was not to hurt the child, but the child is the one who ends up suffering the most. If parents are more aware of this dynamic, they can play a crucial role in promoting healthy parent-child relationships with lasting positive effects.

Incarceration is another reason for the father's absence. He may have been incarcerated during his child's birth and part of their upbringing. Just because he committed a crime doesn't take from the fact that he is his child's biological father and may want to have a relationship with his child. Unfortunately, people get caught up in their circumstances and make mistakes in their lives. Committing a crime doesn't prevent him from being a loving father. Incarceration does not need to be a barrier to a child's relationship with their father. One cannot assume that committing a crime automatically makes him a horrible person and is not worthy of enjoying a paternal relationship or his child's love. I learned that my biological father, Robert Parker, who I will be referring to as "my father" from this point in the book, spent some time incarcerated for committing a crime. He shared that he accepted Christ and completely turned his life around. He even later became a Deacon at his church. Anyone can make a positive change in their life.

Fathers can also be absent due to having drug and alcohol issues. I mentioned how people get caught up in their circumstances. Perhaps, the father became involved in the use of drugs or alcohol and developed a habit. Substance abuse impairs judgment, harms one's life, and impacts the entire family. Although he may have had this issue since the child's birth and possibly during the early years of his child's life, this does not mean he is currently abusing substances. He may have overcome his struggle with substance abuse and perhaps cleaned up his life. Such as the case with my father. He told me he was an alcoholic. I learned from him and my paternal sister that his alcoholism had a significant negative impact on his family. I was fortunate and blessed that he had overcome his alcoholism when I met him.

Some fathers struggle with mental health issues, which can affect their presence in their child's life. If he has a psychotic disorder like schizophrenia or experiences severe depression, he may have spent a lot of his time receiving inpatient services or was mentally unavailable. These disorders can be debilitating and cause a low level of functioning for the individual. Nonetheless, he is still a father. And although it may be challenging, a child can still have a relationship despite his father's mental condition.

Some fathers may have occupations, whether glamorous or not, that take them away from their families for periods of time, causing them to be absent from the home. For example, they may be serving our country in the military. Although this is an admirable reason to be away from the family, this will still impact the child as the child will be in a single-parent home for a significant period of time. Perhaps he is a truck driver or maybe even a celebrity. In these situations, however, the absence is temporary. Unfortunately, he may be absent during a crucial time of the child's development. The father's absence can impact the child if he doesn't contact them consistently or the mother doesn't allow consistent communication with the father while he is away.

Jobs that cause fathers to be away from their children create a void in their children's life. Unfortunately, fathers are unaware of how their absence impacts their children. The difference in these situations is that the father is partially present, most likely providing financially. Since the child is aware of their father, the impact may not be as significant compared to a child who has never met their father.

A less common reason for an absent father is that the mother conceived through artificial insemination. In this case, the mother had no intention of involving the child's father from the get-go. She made a lifestyle choice to fit her needs and did not consider how her decision would impact the child. In this case, finding the father in order to start a relationship would be difficult due to the anonymity of the sperm donor. But thanks to DNA tests and the internet, even a child conceived in this way can track down their father.

It is also possible that the mother became pregnant after someone raped or molested her. In such a case, it is understandable that a mother would want to keep the truth about the biological father hidden, but the child will still wonder about their father.

Perhaps, the absent father doesn't know how to be a father. He may have had an absent father and did not have a role model to emulate. If his father wasn't present, how would he learn to be a father to his child? Maybe his upbringing influenced his decision to become absent. Perhaps he grew up in an abusive or neglectful environment. Possibly, a court dependent and grew up in the foster care system, bounced from one home to the next. These circumstances would impact his ability to be a father.

A father may be absent because he is deceased. He may have passed away before his child's birth, shortly after, or during their upbringing. If he passed away before his child's birth, the child's curiosity is all they have. They will never have the opportunity to ask their father questions in person and have a relationship with him. The child now has to rely on getting information from their mother and others who knew him. If the father passed away during the child's upbringing, then at least the child had a chance to spend time with him.

They spent part of their life with him, even for a short time. Nonetheless, the child does have the opportunity to come to peace with his father's absence.

Even though the book focuses on physically absent fathers, I must acknowledge that some fathers can be physically present yet emotionally absent. This situation is also considered a father absence. The father and child don't have an emotional connection due to not knowing how to communicate with or show affection towards each other. Maybe he is physically present but emotionally unavailable to his family due to his circumstances. This type of father absence also harms a child's psyche and has long-term effects on their adulthood.

Despite how absent fathers are negatively portrayed in the media and frequently referenced in movies and television shows, the bottom line is that a child needs a father. Fathers are just as important as mothers and play a crucial role in their child's emotional and social well-being.

Acknowledgement

I want to first thank my God for ultimately inspiring me and blessing me with my personal, spiritual, and professional experiences to write this book.

To Michael Daniels, for being an admirable husband and foundation for me, supporting me throughout my career, being an excellent example as a father, and demonstrating healthy relationships with our children. To my kids, T.J (thank you for designing the book cover), Jazmyn, Alyssa, Xavier, and Elijah, for demonstrating how a healthy father-child relationship is supposed to be. To my mother, Vicky Rose, who has always been there for me and is a loving and supportive mother. To my grandmother, Margaret Gunn, my second mother, and to Dorothy Cheeks, who were instrumental in connecting me to my birth father. I would have never met my father if it were not for them. To my brother, Nasir Rose, who encouraged me that there was a need for my book since he has friends dealing with this issue.

Cousin Christine Harris, for keeping me connected to my paternal side of the family. The Roses, Moores, Hewletts, and Belts, for accepting and loving me as if I was born into the family. My "bestie," Marleena Rogers, for being my best friend for over four decades and who listened to me read every letter and helped me through the reunion experience. To Robin, Ramadii, and Raseem, for accepting me as their sister and being a part of my life. To Renee for being supportive of my relationship with Robert. To my current pastor, Harry Bratton, and former pastor, Wayne C. Cooper, for contributing to my spiritual growth.

To my friends; Jason Edison, James Dennis, Christopher Davis, and Debriance Walker, with whom I had many conversations about their absent fathers and inspiring me while writing the book. Paul Gibson, for your encouragement and for giving me the book *He Knows My Name*, which inspired Chapter seventeen. Ralph Kuechle, for your support and encouragement while writing the book. Juuna'e Dai'Re for motivating me to complete this book after several years and get it out to the world. Finally, all the years working in foster care and mental health gave me evidence of the damaging effects of having an absent father.

Introduction

Are you an adult dealing with the wound inflicted by your absent father? Do you have unresolved resentment? Do you wonder about your absent father? Have you ever wished he was in your life? Do you need closure? It's not your fault that your father physically or emotionally abandoned you. Children of absent fathers consequently become victims of circumstance. When the father is not present, it creates within the child a void.

In this book, you will learn ways to heal this fatherless void. The self-assessments and the exercises, which you will complete at your own pace, are designed to help you confront and process your thoughts and feelings about your absent father. Purchasing this book means you have acknowledged that not having your father in your life is an issue and, as a result, has affected your life.

Unfortunately, the void doesn't disappear just because we enter adulthood. It stays until there is some resolution. This book will help you to:

- Seek out and reunite with your father or the paternal side of your family, even if your father is unavailable or if it doesn't work out with him.
- Learn information about him that allows you to learn more about yourself.
- Resolve resentment and find acceptance and peace.

Understanding the reasons he is absent and getting his side of the story whenever possible can help one deal better with the situation and, thus, start healing the void.

Of course, some fathers intentionally choose not to be involved in their child's life. Often, however, fathers do not always choose to be absent, contrary to what the media portrays. They may be absent due to circumstances that are outside of their control.

Except when the father is deceased and artificial insemination, an effort needs to be made by both parties to foster and maintain a relationship. Even if the child found out that their father wanted nothing to do with them at the time of their birth or upbringing, circumstances may be different now, and the father may be ready and willing to have a relationship. He may not be able to make up for the lost time, but if you have an opportunity to have him in your life either again or for the first time, he can be there for you in the present.

I was a child who grew up without her biological father and met him for the first time when I was twenty-three years old. My personal experience with this issue inspired me to write this book. I hope that the first-hand experiences I share throughout this book, over twenty-seven years of clinical knowledge, expertise, and my spirituality will help you resolve this issue in your life.

Typically, it is the expectation that the parent should initiate repairing the relationship, but the reality is that this may never happen. My book is about empowering you to take control and take action. I understand there may be some fears of rejection by putting yourself out there, but trying to improve the relationship will be beneficial to you in the long run. Besides, the main reason for your pain is that you already feel rejected by your father. Why wait around for someone who possibly may not know you even exist to initiate? As I mentioned earlier, this may never happen. That doesn't mean he does not love you. It may be that he believes you do not want anything to do with him, or he might be having some fears of rejection by you. But if you open the door, he may be willing to walk through it. Your healing is essential, and you need to take charge of that; I am living proof of this. My biological father was so glad when I initiated and reached out to him. He instantly had a positive response.

Self-discovery will be an emotional experience. I know this personally and from my years being a clinical therapist and counseling others. I refer to this process as self-discovery because you'll examine your thoughts and feelings, and as you gain knowledge about your father, you learn about the other part of yourself. Satisfying your curiosity about your father will put you on the road to healing your void. How that plays out is up to you and the risks you are willing to take. So, I encourage you to allow yourself to be vulnerable and open to the process of traveling on this journey of healing your void. Are you ready?

1

Support Buddy Contract

The first step I recommend in healing your void is to identify a support buddy. My purpose in including this chapter is to ensure that you have a support system in place as this can be an emotional journey. You may be telling yourself that you don't need anyone in your business and that you can handle this on your own. When you drive your car every day, do you think you will get into an accident? Probably not. It is because you may see yourself as a good driver. Yet, you pay for auto insurance. Why? Just in case, right? Same with medical insurance. You pay this outrageous amount of money every month even though you might be so healthy that you don't even catch a common cold in a year. Why do you pay the monthly premium? Just in case, right? Hopefully, I am making my point.

Well, it is beneficial for you to identify a support buddy just in case. You may ask yourself, "Why do I need a support buddy?" It is beneficial to have a support buddy while going through this process to have someone you trust to talk to when you experience intense emotions. Also, you will have someone by your side when you don't know how to move forward. It would be good to have a buddy to discuss your thoughts with or help you search for your father.

You may experience frustration, anger, sadness, gladness, or confusion. The list of feelings can go on. The process will be intense, and you will need support along the way. I wouldn't feel right not recommending this option to you. Going through this process is a huge step you are taking that could potentially change your life forever. My best friend was my support buddy. It helped a lot to have her there for support from the beginning of the journey to seek my biological father until the end when he passed away. So, I believe it is better to have one and not need one than to need one and not have one available to assist.

The first thing I need from you is to brainstorm who you trust in your life. The list can include family members, your best friend, your pastor, or anyone important to you who you believe can support you. The list can be as long as you like, but we want to narrow it down to one person you trust. Perhaps, you may already have that person in mind.

Consider involving people who can be neutral about your situation and will support your journey. Surprisingly, this may not be a family member as they may not be able to be objective if they perceive your father in a negative light. This person will play a crucial role for you in the journey. So, for example, you wouldn't want to pick your mother to go to if you know that she feels some type of way about your father. Doing this will be counterproductive to your healing process.

Specific chapters will recommend buddy checkpoints to prompt you to talk to your buddy based on the heaviness of the material presented in that chapter. Remember, you can check in with your buddy at any point.

Think of this person as your lifeguard when you start drowning in your emotions and doubts. This person can come to rescue you out of the water and resuscitate your motivation by encouraging you when you feel like quitting. As I mentioned previously, self-discovery can be an emotional experience, so having a buddy with you on this journey will make it more bearable. Now, let's get started with that list!

Exercise 1: List of People I Trust

Instructions: write the names of people you would consider being your support buddy throughout this process (if you already have someone in mind, then you can skip the list).

People I Feel Connected To-List

1.
2.
3.
4.
5.
6.
7.
8.
9.
10.

Now, I need you to narrow the list down to three people you trust and write down the individuals' names.

Names

1. _____
2. _____
3. _____

Next, I need you to narrow your list to one person, and how they can help get you through this process.

Name of Support Buddy

1. _____

How They Can Help

1. _____
2. _____
3. _____

The individual listed above is the one you will be going to when you're having difficult moments during this process and need someone to confide in and support you. The purpose of identifying one person to fulfill this role is so that you can have that consistency. This person will be dependable support for you throughout the entire journey and will be in tune with everything you are going through, every step of the way.

Next, you will have that person complete a Support Buddy Contract so that they are aware of their role in this process, and agree to provide you the support you need at any time.

Support Buddy Contract

I_____ have made the decision to work on healing my void of father absence. I understand that this may be a difficult process. Therefore, please assist me by being available if I need someone to talk to, and please encourage me during this journey.

I_____ agree to assist you by being available to talk to and provide encouragement along this journey. You may reach me at the following phone numbers:

1._____
2._____

My signature_____

Support Buddy's signature_____

In addition to having a support buddy, you will also need coping strategies to help you manage your emotions along the way.

2

Emotional First Aid Kit

Y ou will most likely reach for your first aid kit if you have a sudden injury. There is a strong possibility that going through this self-discovery process may trigger deep-seated emotions, bringing them to the forefront. Sometimes, these unexpected emotions can be overwhelming. In the previous chapter, you identified a support buddy. Since this person may not always be available, you will need something to help you manage your feelings immediately.

It will be beneficial to have your emotional first aid kit in place before you delve into this process. What coping strategies have you used in the past that helped you effectively manage your intense emotions? These belong in the first aid kit. Below are some ideas for coping strategies:

- The 4-4-6 deep breathing technique (inhale for four seconds, hold for 4 seconds, and exhale slowly for six seconds for 3-5 minutes)
- Try contacting your support buddy
- CALM app
- Headspace App
- Mindfulness (pick an activity like showering, eating, etc., engaging as many of the five senses as possible, and when your thoughts wander, notice and don't judge them, just bring your focus back to the activity)
- Use a visualization

- Journal
- Engage in your hobby (i.e. gardening, painting, crafts, puzzles, knitting, working on cars, etc.)
- Clean
- Exercise
- Adult coloring book
- Listen to music
- Play with your pet
- Go for a walk
- Read
- Take a bath
- Use essential oils
- Watch your favorite television show, movie, or funny videos

Emotional First Aid "Supplies" (Coping Strategies)

I will use the following "supplies" from my emotional first aid kit when I am feeling emotionally overwhelmed:

1._____

2._____

3._____

I would recommend taking a break from the exercise triggering the emotions, implementing a coping strategy from your first aid kit, and then returning back to the activity when you are ready. The key is to implement these strategies the second you experience these intense emotions. Remember, you are going at your own pace, and can take as long as necessary.

Here is a list of additional resources to add to your kit just in case:

Resources For Additional Support

- Emergency: 911
- National Suicide Prevention Lifeline: 1-800-273-TALK (8255)
- National Hopeline Network: 1-800-SUICIDE (800-784-2433)
- Crisis Text Line (Online 24/7 live messaging): http://www.crisistextline.org. Text "HOME" TO 741741 to connect with a crisis counselor
- American Association of Poison Control Centers: 1-800-222-1222
- National Council on Alcoholism & Drug Dependency hotline 1-800-622-2255
- National Eating Disorders Association (NEDA): 1-800-931-2237
- National Domestic Violence Hotline: 1- 800-799-7233
- LGBT National Hotline: 1-888-843-4564
- Veterans Crisis Line: https://www.veteranscrisisline.net 24/7, confidential crisis support for Veterans and their loved ones. Dial 988 then Press 1, chat online, or text 838255

Now that you have your emotional first aid kit in place, you are ready to explore the emotional connection in healing your void.

3

The Emotional Connection

I nevitably, you will not feel complete unless you have a functional or positive relationship with both biological parents. Or closure regarding the non-existent relationship. I say a positive relationship because you could have both parents physically present and still feel an emptiness due to the lack of an emotional connection or bond. Just merely knowing that someone exists is not enough.

For myself, initially, all I felt I needed was to soothe my curiosity by simply meeting my father. Once we met, I wanted more. I was craving a relationship with him, and we were both willing to make that happen. Emotionally, I felt fulfilled and complete knowing my father helped me understand myself better. It was like all the pieces of a puzzle coming together. For example, I would often look at myself and wonder from whom did I get certain features? Once I met my father, I saw the likeness between us, and I was hyper-focused on every detail of his being. You cannot blame me. I have been waiting for this moment to meet him all my life. I noticed my hands looked exactly like his, and my nose and ears were similar. Even with my legs and my height, there was some resemblance. I even noticed that my demeanor was somewhat similar to his and that we shared the same interest in working with youth. It was like the void in my heart was starting to close.

But when you have never met nor had a relationship with your father, a void will form and naturally cause you to experience certain emotions. Some may experience these emotions more intensely than others, based on the circumstances regarding their father's absence. Perhaps you may have known your father but had a strained relationship due to domestic violence in the home, or he abused you. Or perhaps, your parents went their separate ways for whatever reason, and you felt abandoned by him because he appeared to have moved on without you. Or maybe you never knew him, and your heart is full of resentment because he was never around. You feel like he doesn't care about you because he never bothered to take the time to find you.

Regardless of the circumstance, a void is formed in your heart because you lack the other part of you. Perhaps your mother fulfilled both parenting roles. Or you were raised by another family member or another adult. This family structure was not ideal, yet it was the only option for you. Sometimes, there may even be a stepfather or your mother's boyfriend in the picture. In this type of household, it is not uncommon for the child to say: "You are not my real father!" Why do we say that to someone fulfilling the responsibilities that our father should be doing? We say this because there is a void, and that is the void talking. In other words, "I wish my father were here."

People fail to realize that a mother cannot replace a father in the heart, no matter how wonderful the mother may have been while growing up. She could have been available for you twenty-four hours a day and provided everything you ever needed and wanted, but the void will still be there. In other words, your father holds a special place in your heart. It sucks because you are stuck with the emotional baggage that resulted from his absence.

Let me first discuss and normalize the emotions that one may experience when having a fatherless void. Although these feelings I am about to describe come and go throughout your life, this void is a constant. You begin to experience the pain—consciously or subconsciously—in your heart the moment you realize that your father is absent. The seed of these feelings starts to germinate and take hold. Learning about who your father is, forgiving him, and having closure will fill the void.

Individuals who deny the impact of their father's absence are also experiencing the pain of the void subconsciously. In other words, they are unaware that most of their acting-out behaviors are due to this void; they are suppressing their feelings and not acknowledging their pain. I have seen evidence of this throughout my twenty-seven-year career in the mental health industry. Being in a negative emotional state can lead to negative behaviors such as having anger issues, isolation, under and overeating due to depression, putting yourself down, and being a people-pleaser. You may also engage in reckless behaviors such as substance abuse, self-harm, suicidal attempts, and sexual promiscuity—this list can go on. Some behaviors can even lead to involvement with the legal system.

You may be experiencing several different feelings about your absent father, the main feelings that I am choosing to focus on include; curiosity, resentment, and regret. I will address these three since I believe they are the underlying feelings that perpetuate the void.

Curiosity is a state of active interest or genuinely wanting to know more about something. This feeling allows you to embrace unfamiliar circumstances and experience discovery and joy. Curiosity is natural to feel when your father is absent from your life. You want to know about him as his life is unfamiliar to you in some way. I began to feel the void when I was about eight years old; it was when I realized that all my friends had "real fathers" in their lives since birth, whereas I, on the other hand, my new father only came into my life when I was five years old. It was at that moment I started wondering about the other part of me.

I began to have some questions. I wondered about the man that should have been there five years before my stepfather married my mother. Why have I not seen this person? Where is he now? Is he still alive? Does he have a wife and other kids? How does he treat them? Does he know that I exist? If he does, why does he not come to see me? Does he think about me? Does he care how I am doing? Where does he live? How does he look? Do I look like him? Do I take after him? And the list of questions continued in my mind.

If you are in the same boat and wonder about your "real father," you may have had some of these same questions. It is as if he is some mystery man. You do not know much about him. As a result of his absence, you are left to your imagination because you are curious about how life would be with him around. You are curious about how it would be if your worlds collide. You may even create a fantasy of how he would be as a father in your mind as a way to cope. It is complicated.

Even though you may have this underlying resentment towards him—which I will discuss later —you may put him on a pedestal in your mind. A daughter may imagine her father, horse playing with her, and walking her down the aisle on her wedding day. A son may imagine playing basketball with his father or attending all of his games. He becomes a phantom you are chasing, except he does exist. You cannot see or touch him, but you know he is out there. Without first dealing with your feelings about him, it is difficult to predict how you would react if he were to walk through your front door today. This book will prepare you for that moment.

The fact that you are reading this book means that you are curious about who your father is, how he feels about you, etc., and you want to know how to heal your void. If you already know your father, you may be curious why he is not pursuing a relationship since you are his child. Or even how to make it right with him.

Curiosity

Curiosity is like an itch and will not soothe until you scratch it. How do you alleviate curiosity? You achieve this by actively seeking answers to your questions. Like an itch, if you do not relieve it, it will continue to itch. Just like curiosity, if you never ask questions and actively seek answers, it will not resolve. Relieving the itch will lead to experiencing discovery and joy. You will discover who your father is and who you are.

Healing your void is a huge accomplishment and will help you feel complete. It will be like putting that last piece of the puzzle in place. Try to be optimistic as you approach this healing journey to gain something positive from this experience.

Resentment

I could easily say that one of the feelings one has towards his absent father is anger, but that would not be completely accurate. Anger results in aggressive behavior (i.e. yelling, etc.), whereas resentment is a low-grade form of anger that is triggered by perceptions of unfairness, or being wronged in some way. Anger is used to get an individual to back off or submit, while resentment is a form of mental retaliation. Resentment is something that has been lingering over time. In your mind, it is an injustice that your father abandoned you. Since you have had an absent father throughout your entire childhood or most of it, you most likely are experiencing resentment that has developed throughout your lifetime.

You may not have been aware of or understood the reason for the resentment. It was manifesting from the void. Perhaps you internalized it, which has impacted your social and intimate relationships and other areas of your life. The main reason we feel resentment is the simple fact that we feel rejected by our fathers. Individuals with absent fathers may feel this way if they believe their father intentionally abandoned them.

As I already mentioned, this feeling is fostered over time and does not happen overnight. As a young child, others may have portrayed your father in a negative light. It all depends on what you were told about him while growing up. Former president, Barack Obama, had an absent father. He said during an interview with David Letterman: "my mother was very generous in telling stories that put him in the best light and not bad ones, and it was only later that I learned the bad ones, not from her." It would be ideal if mothers of children with absent fathers could do the same as Barack's mother; highlighting the positive qualities of the absent father. Doing this preserves the emotional health as the child will latch on to, and internalize any information about their father. Internalizing the positive messages will minimize the resentment towards their father.

Were you told that he abandoned the family? Did you grow up around people, including your mother and other relatives, saying negative things about him and not realizing you were listening? If this was the case, it is not uncommon.

How could you not have negative feelings about him? Especially if he is not around to debate the topic. He is not there to say he did not do that, so you are left to your imagination about why he is absent. Also, you do not have anyone advocating for his cause or yours, as you may still want to see him.

Other people may not understand why you want anything to do with your father, especially when they think he is a "loser" or a "deadbeat dad." Do not worry. It's normal and natural for you to want to connect with your father. Someone who has not had to experience growing up without a present father will not understand this void you are dealing with. So do not expect them to be sympathetic or empathetic. They may even be critical, but do not allow their opinions to hinder your healing.

Did you personally have negative experiences with him? Did he mistreat you or other family members at some point in your life? Of course, you would be angry at him and have feelings of resentment that you may hold onto for a long time. Unfortunately, these feelings do not negate the fact that he has left a void in your heart.

During my twenty-seven years in the field of social services and mental health, I have seen many children in foster care whose birth parents abused and neglected them. Yet, they still profess their love for and desire to be with them. It is difficult for people who do not work in the mental health field to understand this. They believe a child is better off living with foster or adoptive parents than neglectful and abusive parents.

Unfortunately, the reality is, as I have witnessed throughout my career, many foster, and adoptive parents abuse these children as well. So now, the child is going from one abusive situation to another. In that child's mind, they believe they are better off living with their biological family that they know, love, and share DNA with than living with abusive strangers. No one wants to be in an abusive situation. They want to be loved and treated right. Hence, it is confusing to reconcile how someone, supposedly your protector, is harming you, yet you need protection from them. It is difficult for some people to understand that you still love this person because this situation is complicated. If this is the situation you were in growing up, you had to face the reality that he is still your biological father and that he is a part of you.

Maybe no one ever told you about him, so you had to use your imagination. Naturally, you will blame yourself and start to believe that it is your fault that he is not around if there is no other explanation. You may have thoughts like why does he not want to see me? Am I not lovable enough? Do I not mean anything to him? Is it because of me that my parents are not together? Did he not want me?

Over time, if you continue to have these negative thoughts and believe them, they will foster resentment towards a father you do not know. Unfortunately, you only have one side of the story—yours or your mother's. You may know your father's side of the story if he was in your life at some point, but maybe you do not understand his reasons.

Nonetheless, the fact that he was not involved in your life when you needed him created resentment. This resentment will perpetuate until you resolve these feelings, either individually or with him. No matter the reason, all you realize is how it creates a void within you. In this case, the advantage is that he may still be physically available, and there are opportunities to work out this situation. Later on in the book, I will discuss how to find him and build a relationship.

Regret

Regret is a sense of loss and longing for someone or something gone. A feeling of disappointment or distress about something that one wishes for could be different. Having an absent father is a loss, and you may experience thoughts that reflect your wish for things to go differently. You see, regret doesn't always have to be disappointment about something you didn't do. We usually understand regret as being disappointed in ourselves. I am going to show you another way regret works.

I remember experiencing this when I realized that I had a "real father", and it was at that point that I felt a loss. I did not feel complete because I knew a part of me was missing. So then I began to feel as though I was missing out. I wondered about the type of father he was and if he was giving his love to another family. What about me? I need his love, and he is missing out on

15

these significant events in my life. He does not realize what a good girl I am. He will never know how well I am doing in school.

If you experience regret continuously, it will ultimately lead to sadness due to feeling rejected by your father or missing your father. This sadness can turn into depression and loneliness. You may become isolated, disinterested in activities, have a sense of worthlessness, have sleep and appetite issues, have suicidal thoughts, or develop self-harming behaviors.

Regrets leading to depression and anxiety will also affect your self-esteem if you do not have a positive father figure in your life to counteract these feelings. You will question your sense of self-worth as these thoughts and feelings filter through your entire being until they become the core of who you are. They start to define your perception of yourself and the world around you.

You may have wondered why your father wasn't present in your life. If no one explains why he left, you will draw your conclusions. You may believe he left because of you and then ask yourself questions such as Why didn't he want to be a part of my life? Is there something wrong with me that he didn't bother sticking around? Is it my fault he left? These thoughts will eventually affect your self-esteem, which is how you feel about yourself.

Self-concept, for females in particular, also has to do with self-image, including body image. As a female, believing your father doesn't love you because you're not "cute enough", etc., can lead to developing an eating disorder and becoming obsessed with your weight.

All areas of your life may become impacted—socially, emotionally, and physically.

Fortunately, I did not get to that point because my maternal grandfather and stepfather were positive father figures who stood in the gap and fulfilled my needs. I did, however, have moments where I experienced regret that my father missed out on some momentous events in my life, as I already mentioned. You may be experiencing the sort of regrets that I described above.

So, as you can see, being regretful doesn't always have to be about your regrets for things you wish you had or had not done personally. I am showing you regret in a different light: regretting something that someone else hasn't done for you in your life. These feelings can be overcome by the process of forgiveness, as will be discussed in a future chapter.

Impact on Relationships

Not only will you experience emotions when dealing with your void, but having this void will ultimately lead to impaired relationships. The reason is; your need to feel loved, your fear of rejection, not feeling worthy of relationships, or having difficulty trusting. Being a people-pleaser is not uncommon. You may get involved with others superficially and not genuinely connect to them or isolate yourself to avoid getting hurt. You may even feel that you don't need anyone and are overly self-reliant. Human relationships, however, are necessary to have a healthy life.

When we have appropriate role models in our parents, we have a positive example and influence in our lives. Our parents pave the way for our values, beliefs, conduct, and morals. The positive example we learn from them, in essence, is crucial in developing our self-concept and helps us develop into emotionally healthy and productive citizens in society. And, of course, for this to happen they need to be present.

When a father is actively involved in their child's life and fosters a supportive and affectionate relationship, there are positive outcomes for that child's cognitive and emotional development. Fathers complement mothers in raising children. For example, mothers tend to be more nurturing while fathers provide structure and discipline that challenges the child in such a way that prepares them to excel academically and to survive in the world. Children who grow up with involved fathers are more comfortable exploring the world around them and more likely to exhibit self-control and pro-social behavior. Both approaches complement each other and result in a well-rounded individual.

A son will desire his father's approval and model his behavior after his father. He learns, throughout his life, how to appropriately interact with women by observing his father's interactions with his mother. A daughter, exposed to his characteristics throughout her childhood, will learn what standards to look for in men when she is older. She will look for his qualities whenever she enters into a relationship. She will expect these men to respect her and treat her how her father did her mother.

So, what does this mean if your father was absent? Whether male or female, you were not exposed to these positive and beneficial interactions and, therefore, do not have that model to pattern your behavior after. You may not know how to interact with the opposite sex and now, as a result, have experienced multiple failed relationships.

As a female, you'll find that you're getting involved with the wrong type of guys because your father wasn't there to teach you what qualities to look for or model the appropriate interactions for you. As a female, you may not know how a man is supposed to treat you. You enter into relationships seeking the love that your father never gave to you. You may lack judgment and engage in reckless behavior, like being sexually promiscuous and confusing sex with love, since you don't know what an appropriate intimate relationship is and lack the knowledge of boundaries your father would have taught you. You may also engage in self-harming behavior like cutting or even have suicidal thoughts.

As a female, you will either have trust issues when it comes to males or will be hesitant to get too close to someone to avoid being abandoned again if maybe you were exposed for a short amount of time with your father—he was in your life briefly before he was absent.

If during the brief time that he was in your life, he was abusive, then as a son, you may pattern your behavior after your father and have abusive tendencies. As a daughter, you may be taken advantage of because you are susceptible to entering into abusive relationships.

Perhaps, you were exposed to positive and beneficial interactions inconsistently when your father was in and out of your life. Regardless, the quality of the relationship with your father in your early development will impact your interactions with others, particularly the opposite sex. If he was never in your life, to begin with, then you had no model or pattern to follow, thus, impairing your relationship with the opposite sex. Since we learn through modeling behaviors, as a male, after who are you modeling your behavior? Or you may have had a father figure in your life as a suitable surrogate who fulfilled that need, and you had healthy social and intimate relationships.

In this next section, I have designed an assessment tool called the AFERA (Absent Father Emotional Response Assessment) for your awareness regarding your void and to see where you are emotionally. I have also included my Absent Father Impact Questionnaire to assess the impact that being fatherless has had on your life. The purpose of these tools is to allow you to gain insight and awareness of your emotional state at this point in your life, which will help you in this journey of healing the void. Take whatever time you need to get the most benefit out of this process. There will also be a post-assessment at the end of this book which will determine if there was a change in ratings for the emotional reaction sections after going through the process outlined in the book. Are you ready?

Pre- AFERA (Absent Father Emotional Response Assessment)

Section #1-Biological Parent Relationship History

1. What was the status of your biological parents' relationship at the time of your birth? Please circle one.

Married Separated Divorced Dating Other_____

2. How did you perceive your biological parents' relationship growing up?

3. How did others perceive their relationship?

4. Did you have a relationship with both biological parents as a child? Please describe.

5. If your biological parents were together at one time during your childhood when did the contact cease between them?

Section #2-Your Relationship History

1. Have you ever met your biological father?

2. If you never knew your biological father, were you aware of his existence as a child? If you answered No, skip to section #3.

3. If so, when was the last time you had contact with him?

4. Was the contact positive or negative? Please Describe.

Section #3- Emotional Reaction

Please be honest with yourself when answering the following questions in this section.

Curiosity

I am curious about the following (please circle yes or no):
1. Where is he? Yes No
2. Is he still alive? Yes No
3. How does he look? Yes No
4. Does he know that I exist? Yes No
5. Does he think about me? Yes No
6. Does he love me? Yes No
7. Does he miss me? Yes No
8. Why hasn't he sought me out? Yes No
9. Is he interested in having a relationship with me? Yes No
10. How is his life? Yes No
11. Does he have another family with other kids, and how does he treat them? Yes No
12. Do I look like or take anything after him? Yes No
13. Is my personality similar to his? Yes No
14. Do we share the same interests? Yes No
15. What type of work does he do? Yes No
16. Is he smart? Yes No
17. How is he doing financially? Yes No
18. How are my paternal relatives? Yes No
19. I wonder about my cultural background. Yes No
20. I wonder about my family's medical and mental health history. Yes No

Resentment

I resent my father for the following (please circle yes or no):
1. For abandoning me and not being a part of my life. Yes No
2. For not caring enough about me to have me in his life. Yes No
3. For not showing me love. Yes No
4. For having another family. Yes No
5. For the way he treated my mom. Yes No
6. For the way he treated me. Yes No
7. For my insecurities. Yes No
8. For my deep-seated anger. Yes No
9. For not supporting me financially. Yes No
10. For all the troubles I got into in my younger years. Yes No
11. For my lack of proper upbringing. Yes No
12. For my emotional problems. Yes No
13. For my relationship problems. Yes No
14. For my academic problems. Yes No
15. For not being available to talk. Yes No
16. For making me feel rejected. Yes No
17. For my substance use problems or other self-destructive habits. Yes No
18. For my self-esteem issues. Yes No
19. For my distrust of others. Yes No
20. For not being a positive male role model in my life. Yes No

Regret

I have regrets because of my father not doing the following and for depriving me of some of these things (please circle yes or no):
1. I feel like I missed out on having a father. Yes No
2. I regret not knowing about the other part of me. Yes No
3. I wish he could have been there for the significant events in my life. Yes No
4. For not being the head of my family. Yes No

5. For not being there for my school events. Yes No
6. For not providing for me financially. Yes No
7. For not helping me with making important life decisions. Yes No
8. For not having him as a protector. Yes No
9. For him not seeing me grow up. Yes No
10. For not having him in the same home. Yes No
11. For not seeing my mom loved by a good man. Yes No
12. For missing my birthdays. Yes No
13. For not celebrating the holidays with me. Yes No
14. For not attending my graduation(s). Yes No
15. For not attending my sports events. Yes No
16. For not helping me with relationships. Yes No
17. For not spending quality time with me. Yes No
18. For not being there to talk about my problems. Yes No
19. For not being there to be a role model. Yes No
20. For not being my disciplinarian. Yes No

Desired Outcome (please circle)

1. I have a desire to seek my birth father. Yes No
2. I want a relationship with him. Yes No
3. I believe we are better off apart. I want to learn to cope with this. Yes No

Scoring

Regarding the resentment and regret sections, add the total amount of yes answers out of the 20 queries. Each yes answer is worth 5 points. So, 60 points or higher indicates the need to focus on that particular area as you go through this book.

Absent Father Impact Questionnaire

Instructions: Read each statement below and circle your answer.

1. I feel insecure and have self-esteem issues. I feel like I will never be good enough.

YES NO

2. I sometimes feel sad, lonely, and depressed.

YES NO

3. I am either overly self-reliant or overly dependent on my partner.

YES NO

4. I have experienced unhealthy romantic relationships.

YES NO

5. I have difficulty committing to others in a romantic relationship.

YES NO

6. I socially isolate or form superficial relationships due to fearing rejection and getting hurt.

YES NO

7. I worry about whether I'll be a good parent.

YES NO

8. I am quick to anger.

YES NO

9. I use alcohol and drugs more than I should.

YES NO

10. I cut myself and engage in other self-harming behaviors.

YES NO

11. I have had thoughts of suicide or have attempted suicide.

YES NO

12. I need constant reassurance that I am loved.

YES NO

13. I feel ashamed that I grew up fatherless and blame myself.

YES NO

14. I feel jealous or hurt when I see parents showing love to their children.

YES NO

15. I have trust issues.

YES NO

16. I feel as if I have a void in my life.

YES NO

Women Only

17. I tend to pick partners who are not good for me.

YES NO

18. I look for a father figure in my relationships.

YES NO

19. I was sexually active at an early age. I have had or currently have multiple sex partners.

YES NO

20. I struggle with eating and have weight issues.

YES NO

Men Only

21. I struggle with recognizing my feelings.

YES NO

22. I struggle with emotionally connecting with others.

YES NO

23. I have difficulty being expressive, or communicating with my partner, children, or women in general.

YES NO

24. I have a fear of intimacy, or I am uncomfortable in intimate situations.

YES NO

Scoring

Answering yes to any of the following questions; 3, 4, 5, 6, 15, 17, 18, 19, 22, 23, 24, means your interpersonal relationships are impacted. Answering yes to any of these questions; 2, 8, 9, 10, 11, 14, 16, 21 means your emotional well-being is impacted. It will be beneficial to keep your responses in mind as you go through the rest of the book.

Next, you will see how knowing about your father can contribute to your well–being.

4

The Genetic Connection

I t is beneficial to know your family history. Learning about your background will help you understand yourself better. That is another reason to learn about your father.

Family Heritage

Family heritage is a person's unique inherited sense of family identity. If you have never met your biological father, you only know half of your family heritage. Learning family stories by conversing with your father and paternal relatives can help you learn about their family traditions, culture, and values. This information will allow you to discover more about yourself, gain a sense of family connection, and pass it on to future generations.

Medical Conditions

Have you ever been unsure what to put for your father's history on a family medical history questionnaire? Or even wondered if, out of that long list of medical conditions, it could be possible that you do have a family history of one of those conditions? I know there have been many times—before meeting my father—that I wondered whether or not one of these conditions runs in my family. I wouldn't know it.

Since you and your father share the same genes, it is good to know of any medical conditions that may run in his family. After all, if you are fortunate enough to meet your father, you also gain an entire paternal side of the family. That means you can find out about any medical conditions that may run on the paternal side of your family and determine your risk and that of your loved ones for a particular medical issue. That is the importance of learning about your family's health history.

A family health history is a record of diseases and health conditions in your family. I mentioned earlier that you share genes. You may also have behaviors in common, such as exercise habits and what you like to eat. You may live in the same area and come into contact with similar things in the environment. Family health history includes all of these factors that can affect your health. It can identify people with a higher-than-usual chance of having common disorders such as heart disease, high blood pressure, stroke, certain cancers, and diabetes. A combination of genetic factors, environmental conditions, and lifestyle choices influence these complex disorders.

A family health history also can provide information about the risk of rare conditions caused by mutations in a single gene, such as cystic fibrosis and sickle cell disease. If you have a family health history of a chronic illness like cancer, heart disease, diabetes, or osteoporosis, you are more likely to get that disease. Share this with your doctor, so they can help you take the measures to prevent any disease and spot it early if it develops.

Knowing one's family health history allows a person to take steps to reduce their risk. For people at an increased risk of certain cancers, healthcare professionals may recommend more frequent screening (such as mammography or colonoscopy), starting at an earlier age. Healthcare providers may also encourage regular checkups or testing for people with a medical condition running in their families. Additionally, lifestyle changes such as adopting a healthier diet, regular exercise, and quitting smoking help many people lower their chances of developing heart disease and other common illnesses.

The easiest and most accurate way these days to get information about family health history is to use DNA Genetic testing to learn predispositions and your chances of developing certain health conditions. Ancestry.com (https://www.ancestry.com/), 23andMe (https://www.23andme.com/), and MyHeritage.com (https://myheritage.com) are the top three rated services you can look into for this. I will discuss these further in Chapter twelve.

Another option, especially if you are on a budget and would prefer to get free information, is to talk to your father or paternal relatives about their health. If you get the opportunity to meet some of your paternal relatives, ask them some questions. Take time to ask them about their medical history and the medical history of those who have passed away. I would encourage you to ask if they had any health problems and when did they occur? A family gathering could be an appropriate time to discuss these issues.

Fortunately, I learned that my two half-sisters had lupus. I couldn't help but think that perhaps this runs on the paternal side, as it seemed coincidental that they both had it. I wasn't sure there was a genetic connection. So it made me wonder if, while in my early twenties, there was a chance that I get this too. Becoming aware of this possibility informed me that I might be at risk of getting this disease, and I educated myself on the condition.

Unfortunately, I didn't take full advantage of asking about my family health history from my father; I took it for granted, thinking I would have many years to have these conversations with him. It turned out that I only had five years with him. I recommend you take advantage of the opportunity to gather as much information as possible from your father and paternal relatives.

Additionally, obtaining medical records and other documents (such as obituaries and death certificates) can help complete a family health history. It is crucial to keep this information up-to-date and share it with a healthcare professional regularly.

The Office of the Surgeon General website offers a tool called My Family Health Portrait, which allows you to enter, print, and update your family health history.

Mental Disorders

Not only do medical conditions run in families, but certain mental illnesses also do. One day, genetic research may make it possible to provide a complete picture of a person's risk of a particular mental disorder or to diagnose it based on their genes. For example, recent NIMH (National Institute of Mental Health)-funded research has identified five major mental disorders—autism, attention deficit hyperactivity disorder, bipolar disease, schizophrenia, and major depression—that share genetic components. If you believe any of these mental disorders run in your family and would like more information, I recommend visiting the National Institute for Mental Health website at (https://www.nimh.nih.gov). It provides an overview of the disorder, its causes, symptoms, and treatment.

If you have a mental illness in your family, you may want to consult a mental health professional who can help you understand risk factors and preventive ones. The NIMH Help for Mental Illness web page (https://www.nimh.nih.gov/findhelp) provides several resources for finding immediate help, locating a health care provider or treatment, and participating in clinical trials.

So, this chapter was to encourage you to be aware of the benefits of taking advantage of asking your father and or paternal relatives about your family medical and mental health history, and not to give you an in-depth lesson on medical conditions and mental disorders. The links I provided give accurate and sufficient information that you need to be well-informed. I hope that you take advantage of the opportunity to ask about your medical and mental health history so that you can know your risk and the risk of your offspring and be proactive in taking steps to minimize those risks.

Now, are you ready to start confronting some of those feelings?

5

Letter to My Father #1, Uncensored- Identifying the Void

Having an absent father is unfortunate, and as I mentioned before, you start to feel the void once you realize that your father is not in your life. Curiosity is normal. As I said earlier, I began to feel the void when I was about eight years old; when I realized that all my friends had "real fathers" that was in their lives since birth, whereas I had a new father who came into my life when I was five years old. It was that moment I started wondering about the other part of me.

Perhaps you feel resentment towards your father and have a more blaming attitude. You may even feel regret about all that he missed in your life. I also experienced this. We discussed curiosity, resentment, and regret in Chapter three. Regardless of how you feel, you have some feelings about his absence from your life. In this activity, the letter serves as an outlet. The fact that you purchased this book implies that you must have feelings regarding your father that you want to work out. Welcome these feelings. Don't hold back. Are you ready?

Exercise: Letter to My Father

Instructions: Use the space below to write an uncensored and unfiltered letter to your father. Also, try to imagine your younger self, and write about what you needed from him growing up.

You can refer to him as whatever you would like. You may not be at the point where you could call him "dad." That is OK. That may even present a conflict within you of what to refer to him as. You can refer to him by his first name. Since this letter is supposed to be unfiltered, you may even call him out of his name (i.e., jerk, etc.). The purpose is to get out your raw feelings. And remember, no one else will see this. Permit yourself to write your secret thoughts.

Remember, no one will be reading this letter, but write it as if you were giving it to your father. This letter provides an opportunity to vent about your father as if you could say these things to him. You can get out all the bitterness you bottled up inside that you have not released. There is an additional letter template if you want to write a letter to your mother; if you have resentment against her. Take all the time you need for this letter; there is no rush. Feel free to add additional sheets if necessary. After you write the letter, feel free to leave it in this workbook. Or tear it out, cut it into small pieces, or burn it. It is up to you. Ready?

Dear_____,

_____

_____

_____

_____

_____

_____

_____

_____

_____

_____

_____

_____

_____

_____

_____

_____

_____

Exercise: Letter to My Mother (optional)

Dear_____,

_____

_____

_____

_____

_____

_____

_____

_____

_____

_____

_____

_____

_____

_____

_____

_____

_____

_____

_____

_____

_____

_____

_____

_____

_____
_____
_____
_____
_____
_____
_____
_____
_____
_____
_____
_____
_____
_____
_____
_____
_____
_____
_____
_____
_____
_____
_____
_____
_____
_____
_____
_____

A Father's Perspective

Now, here is an excerpt from a letter written by my father to me, expressing his feelings.

"I'm not perfect, but I do believe that all children granted to a man and a woman are a precious gift from God. So whether we have maintained a lifelong relationship or one that has just begun, I believe that God has done what he so pleased. You were on my mind and heart many a day over the course of your coming into the world and then being absent from mine for so many years. Some things a man has no control of, and many times I was puzzled as to right and wrong thing to do."

I included this excerpt from my first letter from my father as an example of thoughts an absent father may have about being from his child's life. Later in the "My Reunion" chapter, I will include the entire letter. I wondered throughout my life if he even thought about me. But based on what he wrote in this letter, he did wonder about me too. That may or may not be your experience, but you won't know unless you meet him and talk to him about it. This letter was only the first of many letters and was a way to get to know each other.

Debriefing Exercise

1. How was that experience for you? Was it challenging to think of what to write in the letter? Or was it easy and free-flowing?

2. Were your feelings easily accessible, or did you have to dig deep to reflect on them?

3. Did you find that you ran out of things to say in the letter, or did you fill up the lines provided and may even need to use additional sheets of paper?

4. What would you say was the overall tone of your letter?

5. Describe your emotional state before, during, and after writing the letter?

Buddy Checkpoint

Consider checking in with your buddy if your emotions ran high from this exercise.

In the next chapter, you will be doing some feelings work related to your letter.

6

Identifying Your Feelings

J ust because you experience negative feelings such as anger, sadness, self-pity, or disappointment does not mean feelings are "bad". If you have difficulty tolerating feelings, you may be judging yourself for having feelings or have a negative belief about feelings. The reality is that feelings are just feelings, and they pass. If you reframe how you perceive feelings, you will be able to tolerate them better.

Consider feelings as useful information to assist you in how to act in your situation. In the last chapter, you were able to use letter writing as a dumping ground for your raw feelings. In this chapter, you will clarify these feelings. Remember, your feelings are always valid, so embrace them and don't judge yourself for having them.

Exercise: Feelings About My Father

Instructions: Use the space provided below to write down all of the feelings you are able to identify from the letter you just wrote in Chapter five. Feel free to add more than ten if you need to.

1.
2.
3.

4.

5.

6.

7.

8.

9.

10.

Next, I want you to write each feeling again, but this time, explain why you have this feeling.

1.

2.

3.

4.

5.

6.

7.

8.

9.

10.

Finally, I want you to review these feelings and consider what useful information these feelings are giving you.

_____

_____

_____

_____

_____

_____

_____

In the next chapter, you'll learn how to effectively include your mother in this journey.

7

Dealing with the Mom Factor

There is no doubt that your mother knows the most about the situation, as she was in a relationship with your father and knows the circumstances firsthand regarding his absence. Ideally, she would be the best person to go to for information about your father since she knows him, even if it was a one-night stand. She would know something about your father unless, of course, a total stranger sexually assaulted her. In this case, asking about your father would bring up traumatic memories for your mother.

You may already know how your mother feels about your father, whether negatively or not. She may even feel indifferent about it. My parents didn't end on bad terms. I would say the contrary since he did ask her to marry him. That seemed like an honorable thing for him to do, but it wasn't what my mother wanted. It could be touchy if they ended on bad terms. However, do not let that discourage you. As I stated before, you need to be willing to take risks to achieve happiness for yourself. Besides, what is the worst that can happen? She might say, "I don't want to discuss him." "I hated your father." "He's a loser." "He's a deadbeat father." That is fine. You may have already assumed this. She is not saying anything you didn't expect her to say.

You may be hesitant to approach your mom—that is, if she is still available—because you may not want to trigger any negative emotions she may have about your father. She may be harboring feelings about him that she never had a chance to resolve. Or maybe, she had a positive relationship with him. You may feel she will not understand why you are inquiring about him now.

Again, there may be some hesitancy on your part as you may resent her since you feel that maybe she kept him from you. The reality is that your mom or anyone else in your family will not understand what you are going through unless they have an absent father. She will not comprehend that no matter how bad her relationship was with your father, you have a yearning to know the other part of you.

Your mother only makes up half of who you are. What about the other half? There is still another half of you that you wonder about. And this feeling will not go away until you either meet your father or, at the very least, learn about him and process these feelings inside of you. Be sure to validate for your mom that wanting to gain information about your father will not take away from her relationship with you.

If you feel comfortable at this point asking your mother some questions about your father, I would recommend that you start there. The worst that can happen is that she will refuse to answer or become defensive, wondering why you are asking about him now as she may have those unresolved feelings about him. If she does not want to discuss you can try other avenues. I will discuss this later in the book under the "How To Be Your Own Investigator" chapter. Remember, your mother was also in the situation with you and will know firsthand about the circumstances. As I mentioned, she is the ideal person to get the information from because she may have had an extensive relationship with him.

Suppose that she grew up with your father or knew him from her school days. Or perhaps she only dated him for a short time. She would still know about him as she was intimately involved with this person. Just because things didn't end well doesn't mean they did not have a meaningful relationship. The drawback is that you will get a biased view colored by her resentment, especially if she and your father didn't get along.

If your mother is still available, how do you pursue this venture of resolving your absent-father issues without making her feel uncomfortable due to her unresolved issues with your father? How do you keep yourself from feeling guilty because she may feel you don't appreciate her for raising you as a single parent all these years?

Of course, you don't want to hurt your mother's feelings. But you are an adult. Your mom needs to understand you need to do this, and it is not about her, although she has a connection to the situation. It is about you and your healing and not letting anything get in the way. First of all, you have to approach her non-judgmentally and non-defensively. Since you may harbor resentment towards your mother because you feel she is responsible for keeping you apart from your father, you will need to try to keep your feelings in check. Hopefully, you addressed this in Chapter five, Letter To My Father # 1, Uncensored. I recommend you prepare before having this conversation with her because you do not want to negatively affect your relationship with her if you are on good terms.

If your mother is supportive like mine was, it can be a positive experience to involve her. My mother and I were on good terms. She answered some questions about him once I mustered the courage to ask her about him, and when I finally met my father, he confirmed what she had told me. Feel free to ask your mother all the questions you have been curious about over the years. Start by asking her some of the questions from the AFERA, the self-assessment tool you completed in Chapter three. If you and your mother are close, this will be a free-flowing and natural feeling conversation once you get past your fear of bringing up the subject with her.

What do you do if you and your mother are not on good terms at this time, yet you want this information from her? Keep your goal in mind and how valuable this information will be for you and your healing process. The first thing you need to do is work out the conflict between you and your mother. Use this as an opportunity to fix whatever is broken in your relationship with her. You already have a father absent from your life, so you missed out on that support. Why alienate your mother? Although you may blame your mother for the issue, you are also responsible for your actions and played a part in this. Someone has to make the first move toward resolution. It might as well be you at this time. Besides, you don't want to regret if something unfortunate happened to your mother before you had the chance to make things right.

So, your mother is the key holder of information valuable for your healing journey. Regardless of what terms you are on, if she is still available, approach her and ask her questions about your father in a way that will not damage your relationship with her. Do not take any information for granted. Whatever your mother tells you will be valuable because it takes you one step closer to your goal of healing your void.

Have you ever thought about what you need from your father?

8

Letter to My Father #2- What I Need from My Father

I magine if you had an opportunity to have a conversation with your father. What would you ask of him? I am not talking about material things. For example, information about him so you can satiate your curiosity and get to know yourself better. Also, you may need the story about your parent's relationship and what happened between them. You may need to know about your paternal relatives, half-siblings, etc. You may also want to know about his medical history. Your need could be to have peace with the situation and to heal.

Exercise: Letter to My Father #2

Instructions: Just as you did for letter #1, use the space provided to write a letter to your father, only this time, write about what you need from him. Now that you have emptied all of the bad feelings into letter number one, you can use this letter to focus on what you need from your father.

Take all the time you need for this, as there is no rush. Feel free to add additional sheets if necessary. After you write the letter, you can either leave it in this workbook or tear it out. Unlike the first letter, you may want to keep this one and put it aside. You may need to reference it later if you contact your father.

Dear_____,

_____

_____

_____

_____

_____

_____

_____

_____

_____

_____

_____

_____

_____

_____

_____

_____

_____

_____

_____

_____

_____

_____

_____

_____

_____

_____

_____

_____

_____

_____

_____

_____

_____

_____
_____
_____
_____
_____
_____
_____
_____
_____
_____
_____
_____
_____
_____
_____
_____
_____
_____
_____

Debriefing Exercise

1. How was that experience for you? Was it difficult to think of what to write in the letter? Or was it easy and free-flowing?

2. Did you find that you needed something from your father at this point in your life?

3. If so, did you think of your needs immediately? Or did you have to think about them for a while?

4. Did you find that you ran out of things to say in the letter, or did you fill up the lines?

5. What would you say was the overall tone of your letter?

6. Describe your emotional state before, during, and after writing the letter?

Buddy Checkpoint

Consider checking in with your buddy if your emotions ran high from this exercise.

In the next chapter, you will learn how negative core beliefs are related to negative thoughts.

9

Negative Core Beliefs

O ur underlying beliefs about ourselves, the world, and others shape how we perceive specific situations. These beliefs usually develop due to a negative experience. In your case, your negative core beliefs are most likely due to having an absent father.

These negative core beliefs become activated when one is in a situation that triggers distress, insecurities, or a need for acceptance. Some behaviors related to negative core beliefs include people-pleasing, comparing self to others, and controlling behaviors.

It is possible to change your negative core belief by adopting a new balanced core belief. The belief is balanced because you are acknowledging your challenges or weakness while embracing your strength and hope in the situation.

Below are some examples of negative core beliefs:

- I am worthless
- I am unloveable
- I am a failure
- I am stupid
- I am not enough
- Everything is my fault
- I am ugly

- I will be hurt if I get close to someone
- There is no point in life

Examples of new balanced core beliefs to counteract the negative core beliefs above:

- I am worthy.
- I am loveable just the way I am.
- I do the best that I can.
- I may not be strong in some subjects, but I am good in others.
- I am always doing my best to become better.
- Sometimes I get it right.
- By loving myself, others will love me too.
- Sometimes I will make a good friend.
- I am powerful and can influence my life.

Exercise #1: Identifying My Negative Core Beliefs

Instructions: In the space provided below, reflect and identify as many negative core beliefs as possible.

1.
2.
3.
4.
5.
6.
7.
8.
9.
10.

Exercise #2: Evidence to Support My Negative Core Beliefs

Instructions: In the space below, provide evidence for each belief identified.

1.
2.
3.
4.
5.
6.
7.
8.
9.
10.

Exercise #3: Evidence Against My Negative Core Beliefs

Instructions: In the space below, provide an alternative perspective for evidence against each belief you identified.

1.
2.
3.
4.
5.
6.
7.
8.
9.
10.

Exercise #4: Advice For A Friend

Instructions: In the space below, write what advice you would give to a friend in a similar situation and who has the same type of thinking about it.

_____

_____

_____

_____

Exercise #5: New Balanced Core Belief

Instructions: Reflect on your new balanced beliefs and write them in the space below. Make sure they are statements that resonate with you so that you can tell them to yourself whenever your negative beliefs are activated.

1.
2.
3.
4.
5.
6.
7.
8.
9.
10.

In the next chapter, you'll learn ways to stop those negative thoughts you may be struggling with about your father.

10

Transforming Negative Thoughts

Automatic negative thoughts derive from your underlying negative core belief. This belief is the lens you use when viewing your situation and acts as a mental filter that may cause you to think negatively and lead you to assume a negative outcome. Thinking this way imprisons your mind and can lead to depression, anxiety, and even behavioral reactions. Therefore, how you view this situation will determine whether you can deal with it painfully or successfully. It is common and understandable to have a negative standpoint about your father's lack of involvement in your life. A goal for you in this chapter is to help you transform those negative thoughts into more productive, positive, peaceful ones.

The key is to recognize your cognitive distortions or irrational thought patterns. I believe there are cognitive distortions that one may be dealing with regarding having an absent father. Some include; jumping to conclusions, personalization, blaming, and "should" statements. You may have experienced at least one of these cognitive distortions at one time or another.

Jumping to Conclusions

Jumping to conclusions refers to the tendency to be sure of something without any evidence at all. We have it in our minds that a situation will turn out a certain way. Predicting the future falls under this distortion. This type of thinking is when we assume what will happen with a negative bias instead of recognizing the uncertainty of the situation. For example, say you are thinking, "If I seek out my father, he is going to reject me." Let's take a look at this statement. There is a plan to do something about the situation, but the negative bias causes you to believe the worst-case scenario. You already have it in your mind that it will have a negative outcome. Other examples of jumping to conclusions are; "He hasn't tried to contact me because he doesn't want anything to do with me." "It's because he has a new family." "He doesn't care about me." These conclusions are just assumptions on your part and are not proven facts.

This type of thinking will impede your efforts and motivation to seek out your father and build or improve your relationship if you don't believe it will work out. You will not give him a chance in your mind to redeem himself and don't allow for the possibilities that can happen. We have determined the outcome already before we consider the facts of the case or rationally consider other factors.

Personalization

Someone engaging in this type of distorted thinking may see themselves as the cause of some unhealthy external event they were not responsible for. It is attributing your father's absence to having something to do with you when, in fact, it most likely has nothing to do with you. Instead, it has to do with his or your mother's circumstances. Remember that you are not to blame for what happened, including your father's absence. It was out of your control.

Blaming

Blaming, the opposite of personalization is also a common thought distortion where we hold others responsible for situations that happen to us. We blame others for what goes wrong. The reality is that we are accountable for the way we act and feel. However, it makes us feel better when we can shift the blame and take that pressure off ourselves. The concern with this type of thinking is that we are not addressing our problems if we attribute them to someone else, so the pain is perpetuated and never resolved.

You may tend to blame everything unfortunate in your life on your absent father. He is an easy target. He is not available to defend himself or to contradict your belief. For example, "I could be a better person if it wasn't for my father." "I would have gone to college if it wasn't for my father," "My father is the reason for all my failed relationships," etc. It is true that having an absent father placed you at a disadvantage while growing up and significantly impacted your life, but you must take responsibility for your actions. No one can make you do anything but you. For example, if you touch a hot stove and are burned, how is this your father's fault? It's not. That is how irrational this type of thinking is.

"Should" Statements

"Shoulds" refer to the implicit or explicit rules about how we and others should behave. "Should" statements are the belief that things should be a certain way. You may believe that you "should have done better," "should have worked harder," etc. As far as your father is concerned, you may think that your father "should" have been in your life this entire time. Perhaps, you feel your father "should" have provided financial support while growing up or that he "should" have stayed with your mom; the list can go on and on.

The problem with this type of thinking is that it causes fear or worry and puts unreasonable pressure on you. This way of thinking can make you feel guilty or like a failure. When applying this distorted thinking to your father can perpetuate regret. It's important to realize that one doesn't have control over how someone should act. There is no turning back the hands of time since thinking in "shoulds" isn't going to change your current situation. These are not the facts. Instead, consider the facts and accept the circumstances for what they are. Focus on moving forward.

Hopefully, you can identify with at least one of the distorted thoughts mentioned above and can see how irrational thoughts can affect how we view our situations. The good news is that you can alter these distorted thoughts that get in the way of your peace of mind and healing. I am empowering you to be in control of your thoughts. The following exercises will help you identify and hopefully assist you in altering any negative thought patterns you may be experiencing.

Transforming Negative Thoughts Exercises

Below are four exercises you can do to overcome your distorted thinking regarding your absent father. Fact or Opinion, W.B.M. (Worst, Best, Most Likely) Scenarios, Rewrite with Balance, and Visual Imagery.

Exercise #1: Fact? Opinion?

The difference between a fact and an opinion is that facts can be proven, whereas opinions cannot be. You can't get around the facts, but you can modify opinions. Sometimes, we mix up the two, which distorts our perceptions and negatively affects our lives. An example of an opinion is telling yourself you are "stupid" or believing others think you are "stupid." Even though they are not facts but your opinions or assumptions, these thoughts about yourself soon become your reality and affect your self-esteem. They can be powerful only if you give them the power by making them facts when they aren't.

On the other hand, say you failed a test. It is a fact because you have the red check marks next to the wrong answers and the big red "F" at the top of the page to prove it.

When dealing with an absent father issue, you naturally have thoughts about him and your situation that you may perceive as facts in your mind, but they are opinions. They may have impacted you throughout your life. The below statements may or may not be directly related to your situation. The point of the exercise is to challenge your thinking to have more balanced thoughts by telling the difference between a fact and an opinion.

Instructions: Please read each statement below and circle whether it is a fact or an opinion. You will find the answer key following this exercise.

1. My father was not a part of my childhood since I was five.

Fact Opinion

2. My father doesn't care about me.

Fact Opinion

3. My mother sabotaged my relationship with my father.

Fact Opinion

4. My father passed away.

Fact Opinion

5. My mother worked two jobs to support our family.

Fact Opinion

6. I am a loser because of my father.

Fact Opinion

7. I never met my birth father.

Fact Opinion

8. My father will never accept me.

Fact Opinion

9. I have two children of my own.

Fact Opinion

10. My life would have been better if my father was in it.

Fact Opinion

Answer Key

1. Fact 2. Opinion 3. Opinion 4. Fact 5. Fact 6. Opinion 7. Fact 8. Opinion 9. Fact 10. Opinion

Exercise #2: W.B.M. Scenarios

Often, our minds go to the worst-case scenarios about a situation. There are two other scenarios to consider: the best-case scenarios and the most likely scenarios.

Instructions: In the space below, write the worst-case scenario thoughts you are currently having about your absent father as well as the two other scenarios.

Worst-Case Scenarios

1.
2.
3.
4.
5.
6.
7.
8.
9
10.

Best-Case Scenarios

1.
2.
3.
4.
5.
6.
7.
8.
9.
10.

Most Likely Scenarios

1.
2.

3.

4.

5.

6.

7.

8.

9.

10.

Exercise #3: Rewrite with Balance

Instructions: In this exercise, you will challenge your negative thoughts by writing down the ones you have about your father. Then, you will write down an alternative perspective.

Negative Thoughts About Father

1. *My father forgot about me.*

2.

3.

4.

5.

6.

7.

8.

9.

10.

Alternative Perspectives

1. *It's possible my father thought about me over the years but didn't know what to do.*

2.

3.

4.

5.

6.

7.

8.

9.

10.

Exercise #4: Visual Imagery

For this exercise, I want you to envision successfully attaining your goal of reuniting with your father. Imagine from beginning to end what this looks like for you.

Instructions: In the space provided below, write down the description of what you imagined. For example, you can write about how you imagine having your first phone contact with your father and your first visit.

_____

_____

_____

_____

_____

_____

_____

_____

_____

_____

_____

_____

_____

_____

_____

_____

_____

_____

_____

_____

I discussed the different types of distorted thinking which occur when dealing with the absent father syndrome; jumping to conclusions, personalization, blaming, and "should" statements. These ways of thinking perpetuate negative feelings and are barriers to your healing. Hopefully, the four exercises for transforming negative thoughts helped you adjust your mindset about your situation and moved you closer to the forgiveness process.

11

The Forgiveness Process

To forgive is to stop feeling resentment towards someone who has wronged you. When you forgive someone, you stop blaming that person. Forgiveness is essential in the process of moving on with your life. Without taking this step, you can never heal the void. The previous exercises have been in preparation for this crucial moment of forgiveness. Are you ready?

Hopefully, you have been able to process your resentment or any other negative feelings about your father or mother through the steps you have already taken. Thus far, you have acknowledged how he has wronged you through the AFERA, and increased your awareness of how this situation has impacted your life through the Absent Father Impact Questionnaire. You have also acknowledged your feelings and worked on adjusting your perspective through the exercises in Chapter ten.

Forgiveness does not have to negate that your father was not a part of your life when you needed him, nor the fact you experienced pain and felt disadvantaged in many areas of your life because he was not around. Forgiving does not mean forgetting the past. It just means to let go of the grudge towards your father or mother regarding the past.

If you are still resentful, please stop here and consider a pros and cons list for forgiving your father.

Pros

1.

2.

3.

4.

5.

6.

7.

8.

9.

10.

Cons

1.

2.

3.

4.

5.

6.

7.

8.

9.

10.

Next, consider what may have been the barriers (i.e. his father was absent, substance abuse, etc.) that prevented your father from being present in your life. Please write some reasons on the lines provided below. If you are unaware of any barriers, you can skip this exercise.

_____

_____

_____

_____

_____

_____

Also, reflect and go back to previous exercises and repeat them to get all the residual negative feelings out. Holding on to this resentment is not profitable for you, as you add an unnecessary burden to your life. Forgiveness will set you free. This statement is a cliché, but it is true. On the other hand, if you feel you are ready to proceed with the next exercise, congratulations! You have made significant progress in your healing journey!

Letter of Forgiveness Exercise

Instructions: Just as you did for the other two letters, use the space provided to write a letter of forgiveness to your father. It is a crucial step. I cannot stress this point enough. I do not recommend proceeding to future chapters if you are not ready to forgive. You need to be at a place where you have transformed your negative thoughts. Only write this letter if you genuinely feel this way. If you do not believe you are at this point, hold off until you feel ready.

Take all the time you need for this letter; there's no rush. Feel free to add additional sheets if necessary. After you've written the letter, you can either leave it in this workbook or tear it out. Unlike the first letter, you may want to keep this one and put it aside. You may need to reference it later if you contact your father and desire to share some of these thoughts from the letter with him.

Dear_____,

_____

_____

_____

_____

_____

_____

_____

_____

_____

_____

_____

_____

_____

_____

_____

_____

_____

_____

Debriefing Exercise

1. How was that experience for you? Was it challenging to think of what to write in the letter? Was it easy and free-flowing?

2. Were your feelings easily accessible, or did you have to dig deep to reflect on them?

3. Did you find that you were already at a place of forgiveness upon starting this letter, or did you have to hold off and reflect upon the previous exercises before starting this letter?

4. Did you run out of things to say in the letter or filled up the lines provided using additional sheets of paper?

5. What would you say was the overall tone of your letter?

6. Describe your emotional state before, during, and after writing the letter?

Buddy Checkpoint

Consider checking in with your buddy if your emotions ran high from this exercise.

Hopefully, you are now at the point where you have forgiven your father, or at least close to it. If so, in the next chapter of this book, you will learn how to find him.

12

Be Your Own Investigator

You do not need to hire a private investigator to find your father or find information on your father and paternal relatives. Try being your own investigator using the methods I will outline in this chapter. You will find that you can locate your father on your own by obtaining information on your father from various sources.

Your Mother

I cannot stress enough that the first person to ask about your father is your mother if she is still in your life. Start with her by asking basic questions like, How did you meet? Where did you meet? Where did he live at the time? Does he still live there now? What was he like? Do I look like him? Do you have photographs of him? Why didn't you stay together? Did you meet any of his family members? Do I have any siblings? Do you know which high school he attended? Did you ever try to maintain contact with him? When was the last time you had contact with him?

As you ask these questions, you will learn things about your father that you probably wouldn't learn from anyone else. After all, your mother has to know a little something about him since they were intimate with each other at least once. Don't be afraid to ask questions. It is the only way you will get information from your mother.

But it is not always easy to ask your mother because she has issues with your biological father. So, then what? Well, do not be discouraged. You ask her the questions anyway because any information from her is better than no information. So make your list of questions; they can include my previously mentioned sample questions that you believe your mother would know about your father and then find the courage to approach her at the right time. The worst that can happen is that your mother may not want to discuss him with you. That's fine because you can try other sources of information.

Maternal Relatives

The next step would be to ask anyone in your family who you think would know anything about your father. You can start with your maternal relatives to see if they were around when your mother was dating your father and ask them some questions. You will be surprised at how much they may know.

If your grandparents are alive, go to them next if you are unsuccessful in your attempt with your mother. They would have been around if your mother was dating him while still living at home. As a matter of fact, in my case, my maternal grandmother was friends with my father's aunt. She was the one who facilitated the very first contact between us. My grandmother became aware that I asked about my father and wanted to meet him while I visited Cleveland. She then informed my father's aunt that I wanted to meet him, and his aunt provided my contact information to him. He was then able to initiate contact with me while I was at my maternal aunt's house in Cleveland. What a small world! This information was readily available, and someone was waiting for me to ask. You should consider if anyone on your maternal side of the family has a connection with someone from your paternal side. That was the case with my grandmother and my birth father's aunt.

Maybe someone even went to school with someone in his family. Also, your aunts and uncles could be a good source of this information. Especially if your mother was close to her siblings and they were her confidantes. She may have shared her relationship details and feelings about your father with them. So do not assume that no one on your mother's side of the family knows about your father. I would thoroughly look into this and exhaust the resources within the maternal side of your family before moving on to other sources. That may be the jackpot of information as it was for me, and there would be no need to go any further. If your efforts are futile with your maternal side of your family, you can try your mother's friends.

Mother's Friends

Suppose you did not hit the jackpot of information from your maternal side of the family. Now what? What about close friends of your mother? They may have been around at the time of your mother's involvement with your father and were probably her confidantes. Perhaps, you may still have contact with them by being friends on Facebook (https://facebook.com) or other forms of social media.

However, it could get touchy if your mother refused to provide you with information. She may see it as you going behind her and pursuing the information that you sought from her in the first place. Try to do your best to avoid or minimize any conflict between you and your mother during this process. Although it may feel awkward depending on your relationship with your mother's friends, keep in mind the ultimate goal, and take the risk for your healing. It is up to her friends if they want to give you the information. Do try to be respectful of your mother's wishes. If she is adamant about you going to her friends for this information, remember there are other avenues you can pursue.

Paternal Relatives

I will not assume that just because your father is not in your life, your paternal relatives are not in your life. In some cases, paternal grandparents, aunts, and uncles still are available to you, even though your father was not. I have seen this dynamic throughout my career. Children were removed from their parents and raised by either maternal or paternal relatives. If this is the case, they would be your first point of contact.

If you have a relationship with some people from the paternal side of your family, then definitely ask them. More so than your mother, they will know more about him—although they may not know his whereabouts at the time. It is also possible they do know his whereabouts. At least, they will provide information about his background, how he was while growing up, his personality, etc. They will also have their version of what happened between him and your mother.

It is worth knowing that when obtaining information from relatives, everyone's story may appear a little different based on their perception of your mother and father's relationship. Listen to all these versions and take the parts of the information that make sense.

The Internet

Back in the day, before the World Wide Web, you would have had to hire someone to find a relative. But not anymore. Thanks to the World Wide Web, you can find anyone. Nothing keeps us more connected than the internet. Social media and people search sites are a way to track down people these days. As long as your father has been online at some point, you should be able to gather some information from online resources.

I want to give you free or low-cost ways to search for your family members. With some patience, you can find the information. There are some sights out there that are not as accurate. Also, you will end up paying monthly fees; no online background check is free. You eventually end up paying something. The more reputable ones allow you to pay month to month with unlimited use of the services, including background checks. They usually tend to be highly accurate, and all of them are confidential. The information they find online is for free, and they compile it. So, if you prefer to utilize a paid background check, I will recommend some in this chapter. Furthermore, if you are on a budget, try using cost-free ways to search for people. If it fits within your budget, there are paid background checks that conveniently compile data from various sources which you can use; they range from $15 to $39.

I recommend putting together as much information about your father as possible before your search, using various sources if you are not using a paid background check service.

Google

Google (https://google.com) is not only free, but it's also one of the world's largest databases of information. You can use Google people search if you are looking to find a phone number or address. You type in the name of the individual and search. If you are familiar with their location you can add that information to your search.

I tested this out and entered the name of a former co-worker who was a good friend, but we've lost contact. The last time I spoke with this person was almost twenty years ago. I was curious about this person, so I put his name and searched; his full address came up. It goes for a place of employment or any other activity with which the person is associated.

A search of this nature will result in information like full name, address, phone number, business information, and other details about the person, which are available online. In addition, Google is one of the best places to start looking for records of all kinds simply because its index is so large and can pull in details and resources you might not have thought to include otherwise.

Online White Pages Directory

The online white pages directory (https://whitepages.com) allows you to find the person you are looking for by searching their name or using other key search options; people search by address. To get more details, you will need to sign up for one of their plans that range in price from $4.99 to $14.99.

Facebook

Facebook (https://facebook.com) is one of the world's largest social networks, with hundreds of millions of people accessing it daily. You can try to search for your father this way. And even if you know one paternal relative, you can look into it and see who their friends are and enter the network of your paternal relatives that way—especially if their profiles are public. But even if they are private and you explain that you are a relative, they will most likely friend you.

People Search/ Paid Background Check Services

Although most of these people finder sites advertise as a free service, they are only at no cost to a certain point. You ultimately will pay a fee if you want more detailed information than what was provided for free. It is ok if you prefer to pay, so you don't have to take the time to search the various websites for information. These people search sites are comprehensive search engines with an enormous database with the records of thousands of people. You can search people using their name or a city or state they may have lived in and find all kinds of information.

These sites do all the detective work for you with high accuracy. The information is from a wide variety of places—from both governmental and non-governmental places. These sources include but are not limited to:

- Birth certificates
- Death certificates
- Voter registrations
- Drivers licenses
- Trademark filings
- Census statistics
- Utility
- Companies
- Unsealed lawsuits or legal actions

- Political campaign contributions
- Sex offender registrations
- Professional and business licenses
- Criminal records
- Real estate transactions
- Marriage licenses
- Online account registrations and profiles
- Forum posts
- Government spending reports
- Business and entity filings
- Credit bureaus

This information is legally obtained and is safe for you to view. Background searches protect privacy rights. People can choose to opt-out of the search engine if they want to. Often, these search engines do not offer the information directly, but you can contact the person through the providing website.

Examples of reputable people search websites include; Been Verified (https://www.beenverified.com), Checkmate (https://www.instantcheckmate.com/), Truthfinder (https://www.truthfinder.com/), CheckPeople (https://checkpeople.com/), PeopleLooker (https://www.peoplelooker.com/) , Intellius (https://www.intelius.com/), and US Search (https://www.ussearch.com/). They charge a small fee ranging from $15 to $39 monthly for you to view a full report. Most include background checks.

Since these searches may bring up every phone number, email address, and residential address your father ever had, you may want to contact all of these numbers to see which one is accurate. How do I know this? I searched, and other people, and every single phone number, including cell and landline, house address, and email address, came up. Scary, huh? Also, some inaccurate numbers came up as well. Do not get your hopes up too high just in case you do not get accurate information. You can check out each one to see which of these best suits what you're looking for.

DNA Test Kits

As mentioned in Chapter four, another way to reconnect with biological family and find closure using DNA test kits. Some may provide some basic information for free. But just like any other people finder resource, to get more information, you may need to get a subscription and pay monthly membership fees as well.

23andMe, AncestryDNA, and MyHeritage are among the world's most well-known and successful commercial DNA testing companies. All three companies will provide a list of their other customers who appear to be your relatives based on your common DNA. To figure out the best test kit for you, visit (https://www.dnaweekly.com/blog/myheritage-vs-andme-vs-ancestry dna/) which compares all three and can help you make a decision based on your preferences.

23andMe

This genetic test gives you a comprehensive ancestry breakdown, personalized health insights, and more. Although 23andMe doesn't have free trials for new customers, it is better if you want to learn more about your risks of developing certain diseases or the odds of passing on health conditions to your children. Also, the ancestry information is richer and more detailed than the other two services. Test kits starting price is $99. To get more information, visit (https://www.23andme.com/).

Ancestry

This genetic test allows you to combine DNA results and an enormous collection of records to help understand your genealogy and to help you find family. The database is larger than 23andMe and has three membership levels. The DNA kit costs $99. For more information, you can go to (https://www.an cestry.com/).

MyHeritage

Like the previously discussed ones, the MyHeritage DNA test kit can help you explore the lives of your ancestors, learn your ethnic origins and find new relatives. The DNA test cost is $59, which is less expensive than the other two. However, they don't prepay postage like the other two services. The membership fees range from free for the limited-family tree to paid memberships. For more information on the different membership subscriptions, you may visit the website (https://www.myheritage.com).

FamilySearch

As a budget-friendly option, you can try out FamilySearch. It is comprehensive and easy to use and doesn't cost anything. Although FamilySearch (https://www.familysearch.org/) is run and funded by The Church of Jesus Christ of Latter-day Saints, the site is for everyone to use. The centers and website are free and open to the public. You can view scanned documents, look up details about your ancestors and build a family tree complete with photos without spending a dime. I would advise you not to get your hopes up for this one. However, it doesn't hurt to try it since it is free. For more information, you can visit the website at (https://www.familysearch.org/).

So as you can see, there are multiple avenues to search for your biological father and paternal relatives. This list of resources that I have provided is by no means exhaustive, but it should assist you in at least getting started with your search. It is possible to find who you are looking for using these sources. You may even ask your buddy to assist you in your search efforts since two heads are better than one.

I found someone. Now what? In the following chapters, I will go over the next step of reconnecting with your father or paternal relatives. You will also have the opportunity to read about my real-life reunion story, and hopefully, this will motivate and inspire you in your quest.

13

My Reunion Story

I decided to add my personal experience of my reunion with my father to give you a real-life example of how a dream of reuniting with your father can become a reality. I hope my experience will inspire you to find and meet your father and have a positive relationship.

The Initial Reunion

I did not know my biological father while growing up. My mother and my stepfather raised me, making sure I had everything. As I mentioned, it wasn't until I was eight that I had a concept of a "real father," as in biological. I noticed the other kids had a father since birth, whereas I had a father who came into the picture when I was five. I often wondered about the other part of me.

I recall finding an old wrinkled postcard about child support when I was eight. It had the name Robert Parker on it. At the time, I was living in an apartment with my mother, stepfather, and baby brother. I assumed this was my father's name on the postcard. I kept this little wrinkled postcard in my possession because it was the only tangible thing I had that represented my father. It became significant to me, even if it had to do with child support services. I don't believe anyone ever knew about this. To this day, I still have this little postcard in my keepsake box.

Since I was aware that my stepfather didn't enter my life until I was five, I knew there had to be a birth father at some point. My mother had a Cleveland, Ohio, telephone book, even though she lived in California. It dawned on me that he just may be listed in the white pages. I opened the book and searched for Robert Parker. There were six Robert Parkers listed. It was tempting to go down the list and call each number, assuming that one of these people was him. I must have gone through this process of opening the white pages and looking at his name about 20-30 times but never dared to call.

Part of me was scared because I was afraid of rejection. I was concerned that he might not even know me. I had a lot of questions in my mind as I stared at his name on the white page. Does he know I even exist? Will he be happy to hear from me? Does he have other kids, and does he even care about me? I would close the book in disappointment feeling sad and angry that he must not know or care about me. Why isn't he asking about me and trying to contact me?

Naturally, I asked my mother these questions. She only answered a few because she didn't keep in touch with him. They were together only briefly, then he proposed to her. She declined the proposal, and then they went their separate ways.

Well, I eventually met my father at the age of twenty-three. As I mentioned previously, my grandmother was friends with his aunt. She was the one who made the reunion possible. I will never forget that day.

It was Christmastime, 1995 when I visited my relatives in Cleveland, Ohio. I was on a mission on this particular trip. I wanted to meet my father. My grandmother let me know that he was going to contact me. I received a phone call from him while staying at my aunt's house. It felt surreal because all these years had passed, yet it seemed simple for us to reunite. The telephone conversation was brief as we made plans to meet in person the next day at my grandparent's house. I wanted my hair to be perfect and wear a nice outfit to make a positive first impression. I had no idea how he looked, so I was anxious to see if I resembled him and if I was the offspring of a handsome man.

It was the next day, and I went over to my grandparent's house. I constantly looked out the window, waiting for him to pull up to get a sneak peek of what he looked like before he could see me. My two aunts, my mother, and my grandmother were also in the house.

As he came through the door, we greeted and hugged each other. My grandmother, mother, and aunts said 'hi,' and left the room so we could have time together. I was surprised at how natural it felt. It did not feel awkward at all. He appeared to be a warm person. We sat on the couch, and I brought out old photo albums my grandmother had of me as a baby to show him. I asked him a lot of questions, and he answered them all!

We spent time talking about our current living situations. I was surprised to hear that I had four other siblings, not including my younger brother, whom I share the same mother with. I found out that I had two older half-sisters and two younger half-brothers.

I was anxious to meet them, yet unsure how we would respond to one another. So my father said he would arrange for him, myself, and my siblings to go to dinner that evening, and then he left. My mother, aunt, and grandmother came out to say goodbye and grilled me on my experience of meeting my "real father" for the first time.

The Big Dinner

The awkward moment was when I was getting ready to go out to dinner and my younger brother, who I grew up with, had no idea that we had different fathers. It was news to him. Also, it was news to me that my cousins were aware of the situation, but it was an awkward moment for them.

My father, half-siblings, and I went to a restaurant called Mountain Jack's, a steakhouse in Cleveland, and this was an even more awkward moment. The meeting with the siblings did not feel as natural as my reunion with my father did. We all felt uncomfortable because they had no idea I existed, so they had questions on their minds. We all hugged each other and then sat down at the table.

I observed and sensed my half-siblings staring at me. I, too, was trying to get a good look at them. We all sat at the table, looked at the menu, and placed our orders. The oldest sister commented on my ordering swordfish. She said that this must be a "California thing."

The conversation went on for a while as we waited for our food and continued as we were eating. Our father asked if anyone had any questions, and the second to youngest brother asked his father if there were any more out there, meaning any more illegitimate children. I found out that the oldest sibling had also recently been reunited with our father only a couple of years prior. So, there is no wonder that the two younger brothers would consider the possibility of their father having more kids out there in the world. The second oldest sister wasn't at the dinner because she was in Washington. Our father assured us all that there were no other siblings out there.

They asked me more questions than I asked them. I felt like I was on the hot seat, but that was fine because they were just trying to get to know me a little bit. The difference between us is that, at least, I considered the possibility that they could have existed, whereas they had no idea that I was out there. So it was a complete shock for them. I, on the other hand, was somewhat mentally prepared because I heard there were other children.

We enjoyed each other's company, and I almost did not want the evening to end. This reunion only whets my appetite, and I was hungry to have more one-on-one time with my father. It wasn't that I did not enjoy spending time with the siblings, but I just felt that it was essential for me to get to know him and bond with him first and resolve the void in my heart before I take further steps in bonding with my siblings and other relatives. After all, my mission for this trip was to meet my father and get to know him.

Where Do We Go from Here?

So now that my father and I are past the big reunion, where do we go from here? Well, we agreed to keep in touch before I left Cleveland. He gave me all his contact information and asked me to use it as I saw fit. So he put the ball in my court to make the next move.

On the plane ride back to California, all I could think about during the five-hour flight was the experience that had happened a couple of days ago. It was all starting to hit me. I just met my father! As soon as I got home, my emotions hit me. I needed to process this whole thing. I couldn't wait to tell my best friend of almost twenty years at the time. It was awkward to be around my stepfather because I was unsure if he knew about my reunion. If he didn't, I surely didn't want to be the one to tell him because I wasn't too sure how he would take it. My mother did inform him, but he didn't say anything to me about it.

I have to admit, from that point on, all I could think about was hearing from my newly found father. I wrote him a letter, sharing my feelings about our reunion. I was then anxiously awaiting his return letter in the mail. I ran to the mailbox daily but did not have to wait long. Sure enough, within a week, I received a letter back. He must have written me the same day he received my letter and taken it to the post office on the same day. I was excited to open the letter because I wanted to hear from him so badly. The letter read:

My Dear Erika, January 9th, 1996

"I was truly glad to hear from you. To tell you the truth, I was waiting for your response to our initial coming together. I needed to know how you felt deep within your heart about me. If you recall, the last thing I said to you was, "you have all my information, and you use it as you see fit." I'm sincerely glad that you cared enough to make the first move toward our coming together as father and daughter. To be honest, I was very nervous and couldn't quite decide what to do next.

The reason I chose to write you a letter instead of calling you on the telephone is that writing, to me, is a much more intimate way of communicating when a person wants to speak from the heart. Impromptu words and feelings are eliminated.

Let me say that you are a beautiful young lady. Both physically and personality-wise endowed. It is no surprise though because you are my blood. And whether it is accepted by others or not, you have inherited many attributes and just who you are from me. I can't help but feel a sense of pride having met you, even if it was for the first time in many years.

I don't want to spend a lot of words in this letter trekking into past events of our eventual destinies and what happened or didn't happen. I'm sure as our relationship grows and we begin to love and believe in each other, the truth about things will surface. These things will come about with in-person conversation. That is the best way.

Let me say this, the one thing that you will learn about me is that I love all my children and will go to any lengths to show that love. I'm not perfect, but I do believe that all children granted to a man and a woman are a precious gift from God. So whether we have maintained a lifelong relationship or one that has just begun, I believe that God has done what he so pleases. You were on my mind and heart many a day over the course of your coming into the world and then being absent from mine for so many years. Some things, a man has no control of, and many times, I was puzzled as to the right and wrong thing to do.

In these stages of my life, I've learned to let go and let God. I feel and honestly believe His all-powerful will has walked with both of us the past 23 years, and 1996 would be as he willed. Us coming together is a blessing from above.

Please don't ever feel like you missed out on anything regarding me as a father. God placed you in very caring hands all these years. Hands that gave you an abundance of love, integrity, respect, and substance. You have a very fine and lovely mother. She has always been that way and I saw much of her in you. You are truly blessed to be her daughter, and again, let me repeat "God's will for us is always done".

I'd better begin to end this letter because there is so much that I want to say. I will answer some of the questions you ask and respond to specifics in your letter.

It is always a blessing to have someone to think of as a best friend, you have two. My specialty around here is barbecuing ribs and I get special requests from the family so you can request barbecue- ribs, steaks, chicken. My wife bakes a delicious peach cobbler. She always gets requests.

Ginger Ale is my favorite soda, everybody knows that. I'm a Marvin Gaye fan from his beginnings. Anita Baker is seriously on the mark with her smooth style.

Your brothers and sisters were very happy and glad for you. Your sister (who was in Washington) could not stop asking questions about you and was sorry she couldn't meet you. My wife loves me and has always wanted the best for me and honestly loves me and all that is me. You are me. She wanted to come to dinner with us, but felt a reunion of just the kids at first would be better. You will have plenty of time to learn and get to know everyone.

Finally, we have to open our hearts and minds and give this relationship a door that will never close. I'm positive love will walk in and stay.

Your father,

Robert.

P.S

Call or write me anytime you feel the need or want to. I will give your address to your two sisters."

This letter was only the first of many letters and was a way to get to know each other. We wrote back and forth to each other for years. We started to become comfortable transitioning from letters to frequent telephone contact. He would send me photos, family videos, and gifts. From this point, he always remembered me on my birthday and Christmas. I wasn't expecting anything from him, just a relationship.

Coming Out to California

We were eager to see each other in person once again, so Robert wrote to me in a letter dated January 31, 1996:

"I don't know how long I can bear this kind of communicating. I realize this writing of letters to one another is a very intimate style of expressing

ourselves, but I thirst to hear your voice or see you in person more and more with each letter.

My cousin works for American Airlines and informs me of certain bargain packages. I know that one day, she will call and tell me about a package to California at the right time so that I can be off work and able to take advantage of it. I've never been to California because I never made it a priority destination, but now I have a good reason to. I'm depending on God to bless us that way. I pray that he will.

So, this became a reality. Robert and his wife made plans to come out and spend an entire week with me in California. He provided the flight information in a letter that he wrote to me in April of 1996:

"P.S. I will arrive in California, Burbank Airport at 3:25 July, 1st flight 1455. As of now, I will stay at the Holiday Inn on 3321 E. Colorado Blvd (may change). Will have a rental car at the airport. I will depart Burbank on July 8th".

They stayed at the Holiday Inn Express in Pasadena, not too far from where I lived, in Altadena at the time. It was awkward when they showed up at my home because my stepfather and mother were there. Awkward because both of my fathers would meet for the first time, and his wife would meet the mother of her husband's long-lost daughter.

It turned out to be alright. My fathers didn't have much to say to each other. Just a greeting. The same with my mother and Robert's wife. They picked me up, went to Universal Studios, and had a blast. It was so awesome to spend time with Robert that week.

We also went to Hollywood, Venice Beach, China Town, and the Los Angeles Garment District. I took him for a drive in the Chaney Trail Mountains in Altadena, and he told me he had never been to the mountains since there are no mountains in Cleveland. I took him to Eaton Canyon, and he was amazed at the scenery in California with the mountains and palm trees. I even took him to Roscoe's Chicken and Waffles in Pasadena, a famous waffle house.

We did a lot together on the Fourth of July. First of all, we went to see the movie *Independence Day*. It would be the first and only movie I ever watched with my father. Robert wanted to visit his cousins while he was in California, and I met other relatives who live in Inglewood. We then went to a cousin's home for dinner. We ended the night by watching the fireworks on The Queen Mary.

My father wanted me to stay at the hotel with them to spend even more time with him. We ate all our meals together, sat in the hot tub, and just talked, talked, and talked. During this time, Robert answered the questions I had about him. I learned about his past and how that affected him in the present. For example, he informed me that he had been incarcerated for a few years and was addicted to alcohol and drugs, but then he eventually received Christ in his life and became a deacon. I also learned that he and I have a lot in common since we work with youth.

One memorable moment with Robert was when he taught me some driving tips, including paralleling parking. It was at this moment I felt he was a father teaching his daughter.

The Most Important Decision of My Life

Even though I only knew Robert for a short amount of time, he profoundly affected my life. He helped me make the most important decision an individual can make; accepting the Lord Jesus Christ.

Here is an excerpt from a letter that reflects how important this was to him.

> *Hi My Darling Daughter, July 17, 1996*
> *"I'm sincerely hoping this letter finds you physically healthy and with peace of mind. Sorry to hear that you caught a cold, and hope you are better and full of energy. You will need all the strength you can muster up to embark upon your new venture in the focus group on youth activities. Just know that through Christ who strengthens you, you can do all things. You'll find that bit of encouragement in the book of Philippians in the 4th chapter of the Bible. Philippians is considered by many to be the*

'book of mental for the Christian'. The words "mind" and "joy" are mentioned a few times.

I was so filled with joy that I almost cried when I read in your letter that you were having Bible study every day after work and plan to rededicate your life to the Church of Christ Jesus. Erika, that is the best decision you've ever made in your life. I don't want to make this letter a sermon, so I'll leave it at that. Nothing would make me happier before I leave this earth to be with the Lord than knowing all my children have accepted Jesus Christ as their personal Savior. As you get to know me more, you will learn about what Christ has done for me, including bringing you back into my life physically. I've had my ups and downs in the 43 years (44 July 14th) I've lived, but God has blessed me."

For years, I attended church and was baptized, but I realized I was not saved. I learned from Robert what salvation was all about, and I did not have that. At some point, he helped me realize that I needed to take this step.

During one of our phone calls, we had a more serious conversation about the status of my salvation, and he guided me to the scripture, Romans 10:9, to read about the fact that I have to admit, believe and confess. After I got off the phone with him, I pulled out this little orange bible that the Gideons handed me back in middle school and read the verse he gave me. It was actually on the inside back cover of the book. I read it aloud, fell to my knees, and prayed. I was crying, and this experience went on for hours. It was as if the Lord was glad that I finally let him into my heart after all the years of knocking on the door of my heart. I felt a sense of peace and somewhat different when I got up off my knees. I then headed to work. From that point, life felt very different. I attribute this change to Robert. He had been priming me since we first met for this moment of acceptance of Christ Jesus into my life.

The Will of God

10/3/98

"Erika, you and I are in the will of God. There is not one soul on earth with enough power to affect what the future holds in this father-daughter relationship. Twenty-five years have passed and I honestly believe that our spirits were mingling with one another for the duration. From birth to the present, I've felt it. I don't know about your spiritual awareness and how deep and sincere, how open and heartfelt, how trusting and abiding the spirit of the Lord dwells within you, but I will not accept the fact that you don't feel anything of a spiritual nature when it comes to our relationship. Everything is going to be alright. Each conference, whether it be by letter, telephone, or telepathy, show you evidence of growth in your Christian walk with the Lord. You are spiritually in tune with reality and yourself, and it grows with each day."

I believe that God's will was the reason for the reunion. From the beginning, I felt that the Lord placed it in my heart at the right time to pursue the reunion with Robert and the Lord who facilitated the process. I felt the Lord's presence throughout the meeting and getting to know Robert. It is apparent he did it too. God often navigates the circumstances so that he can fulfill His will.

The End of Our Journey Together

I became engaged to my husband in October 1997. By this time, Robert and I spoke regularly on the telephone, and our letter writing had turned into emailing each other back and forth occasionally. My husband and I went to Cleveland in July of 1997 for my grandparent's 50th wedding anniversary. I was in for a surprise when I went to visit Robert, and not a good one.

He had been ill for some time. Those years of alcoholism had finally caught up to him in his liver. He needed a liver transplant and was on the list to receive one. During a trip to Cleveland, I had planned on visiting my father. When I called his home to speak to him, his wife informed me that he was in the hospital and was very ill. My husband and I went to the hospital to see him. I was in shock. I was not expecting to see him in this condition. He did not want me to see him like this. He had been like this for a while, but he never let me know when I spoke to him on the phone. He was looking forward to coming out and throwing a barbecue for me. He was still planning this barbecue for me from his hospital bed and was determined to show me a good time in his home with his family, even though he was in the hospital. The barbecue did not happen because it just didn't make sense. I still appreciate his determination to do it for me.

After he left the hospital, he surprised me by driving by my grandparents' house. He did not look the same as when I saw him last in California because he looked sickly and had lost a lot of weight. But it didn't matter to me because I was glad to see him and spend time with him again.

Several months later, as my wedding day approached, Robert wanted to come out to my wedding. At first, all I could think about was the conflict that would cause because my other father would be there. Who would walk me down the aisle? Anyway, I then realized there was no way that Robert would expect to have the honor of walking me down the aisle over my stepfather, who had practically raised me all my life. I would have, however, entertained the idea of having one father on each arm.

Fortunately, Robert had recently received a liver transplant but was too feeble to come out for my wedding. Although he was too ill to come out for my wedding as he had planned, he wanted to help out financially. He paid for my wedding gown and the Limo.

In 2001, he became ill again. His body was rejecting the liver. When I came home from work, my husband asked me to sit on the couch. I knew there was bad news coming, but I wasn't sure. My heart began beating pretty fast as I anxiously awaited news he was about to break to me. I had a seat, and my husband told me that Robert was in the hospital and his chances of survival were not looking good. We prayed that the situation would turn around for him. I tried to have hope that he would pull through this because I wondered why the Lord would give him a liver transplant just to allow him to die.

That was on my mind that entire evening. I finally went to bed, and at approximately 4 a.m., I suddenly woke up and sat on my bed. It felt as though someone had blown the candle out in my heart. That was the sensation that I felt. Then I went back to sleep.

I received a phone call early the next day. It was a message on the voicemail from my sister saying Robert had passed away at around 4 a.m.—that was why I felt that sensation in my heart. It was at that very moment that he passed. Something was going on with the phone, and I didn't receive the call. I called the hospital, and a nurse verified that Robert "expired"—which she put it—at around 4 a.m.

I called my mother and was crying on the phone. And, then I contacted my employer to call off to deal with this news. My husband and I made flight reservations to go to Cleveland to attend the funeral. My church family at the time was great through all this. One of the couples in the church, a reverend, and his wife, assisted us financially by purchasing plane tickets. My husband and I had a seven-month-old daughter, in addition to his son and daughter, my stepchildren. They lived with their mother at the time. My husband, daughter, and I went to Cleveland and stayed with my grandparents. It was the month of January, so there was a lot of snow on the ground.

We went to view the body with my siblings. It was strange sitting there, looking at my deceased father in his casket with my siblings. Oh, how I wished we all could have spent more time together with our father when he was alive and not in this way. It felt surreal.

The next day was the funeral, and I rode in the Limo with my siblings to the funeral. I was able to be seated with the family in the front. Although it was a solemn occasion, it was an opportunity to learn more about my father through the individuals who came up to speak about him. I learned a lot about how he helped people. Afterward, we went to the house and watched a video slideshow of memories. They gave me a copy of this.

Robert's wife and my siblings wanted to honor me because of our recent reunion and the fact that I only had five years with him, allowing me to share a thought in the program. So I wrote in the program:

"Dad, although our time together was brief, you made me feel as if we've known each other forever. Thank you for leading me to the Lord because now, I have the comfort of knowing that we will meet again someday. Love, Erika."

I hope my reunion story was inspirational as you read about creating your own reunion story in the next chapter.

14

Your Reunion & Relationship Building

The Initial Contact

Now, suppose that you located your father. What is the next step? How do you reach out to him? What do you say? If you feel comfortable and have his phone number, you can give him a call. I recommend writing him a letter if you have his address or have some anxiety or fears about this initial contact. If you write a letter, you can put as much thought as you want into what you would like to express to him. I don't mean to send him the uncensored letter from Chapter five. That was an exercise to help you release your negative feelings about him. You want to be kind, sincere, and inviting in this letter. You can start the letter off by saying, for example:

> Dear Dad (or whatever you prefer to call him),
>   It is your daughter/son (your name here). It has taken me a long time to get up the nerve to contact you, but I finally decided that I would like to meet you /be in touch with you again. I want to get to know you and have a relationship with you.

Then, you can tell him a little about yourself and enclose a photo of you (and your family). Wrap up the letter by asking him to write you back and send a picture of himself, and include your telephone number so he can have the option of calling you. That's it. You can keep the letter short or include your life story. It all depends on how comfortable you are. Trust that he will not get bored reading your letter. He has missed out on your life, so this is an opportunity for him to get caught up. I will bet that he will be pleasantly surprised and excited to hear from you. Do not get discouraged if you do not get a letter back from him right away or at all.

After a couple of weeks or so, I recommend calling him on the phone if you have his phone number. You don't want to give up too soon. Often, fathers who have been absent from their children's lives are experiencing guilt and shame, and these feelings may be the barrier to him initiating contact with you. So if you make the first move, based on the letter's tone, this action opens the door and relieves some guilt and shame.

Buddy Checkpoint

I would recommend checking in with your buddy at this point so they can support as they may be able to encourage you to make this initial contact. It may be one of the most complicated decisions you will have to make, as it can be emotional and life-altering if you successfully make contact. It is a crucial moment for you. Everything you have worked on in this book has prepared you for this moment!

The Initial Meeting

Suppose you were successful at having initial contact with him. Congratulations! Now, you can move on to the next step, setting up the initial meeting. It may be the first time you meet or the first time in a long time since you have seen each other. In your first phone call or your first or second letter to him, discuss meeting up with each other. Again, depending on your comfort level, you can meet with him immediately, write back and forth or use your preferred communication for a while before meeting in person.

In my situation, we met right away after the first phone contact. Your father may be excited to see you since either he has never met you or hasn't seen you in a long time. Be flexible either way. When setting up this meeting, make sure it is at a location where you feel most comfortable and will not make others in the household uncomfortable. For example, you wouldn't want to invite him over to your home if you still live with your mother and they are not on good terms. Use your best judgment here. If you feel more comfortable having someone with you, such as a friend, a relative, or your check-in buddy, that would be appropriate. Also, be sure to check in with your buddy throughout this process.

I felt comfortable meeting him at my grandparent's home. Since my mother didn't have any negative feelings toward him. She was present—but in the bedroom—and available for support. You can also meet in the community at a park, restaurant, etc. If you choose to meet at a restaurant, assume you are paying separately. Don't assume that he will pay for your meal because if he doesn't, then you will be disappointed. It will affect your relationship building. If he offers to pay, then allow him to.

Do not be concerned about what to say. You have been waiting for this moment and you're full of questions. You can reference your "What I Need From My Father" letter and forgiveness letters from the previous chapters. Keep it positive and not as an opportunity to make him feel guilty. Remember, you have already forgiven him before this moment. I am sure he will have questions for you as well. Take a deep breath and let the conversation flow naturally. Have the mindset that this is the beginning of your new relationship, and there will be more meetings to come.

Buddy Checkpoint

As I mentioned earlier, I recommend you check in with your buddy after your first meeting as often, as you may need to process the experience and discuss with your buddy what your next step should be.

Relationship Building

Now that you have been reunited with your father, whether for the first time or after a while, you have to ensure that the relationship continues and is long-lasting. Treat this as a fresh start, a clean slate. Keep in mind that it takes effort on both parts to build and maintain a relationship. Furthermore, know that you may not be able to see him as often as you'd like due to distance or other circumstances. In the meantime, below are some ways that I recommend you build and maintain your new relationship.

Focus on the Positives

Whenever you interact with your father, focus on having positive conversations. Ask him about his life, including upbringing, education, career, hobbies, and interests. Below in this section, I have provided a list of questions that can be conversation starters.

The topics are endless, but this list below will be a good start. Remember, you are learning about yourself when you learn about your father. Try to find out about his philosophy on life, religious views, political views, favorite sports teams, etc. Avoid arguments over disagreements about religion and politics, as those can be contentious topics. It is not worth damaging the relationship before it even begins. Just agree to disagree.

Conversation Starter Questions

1. What were the circumstances preventing you from being present in my life?
2. Do I have any siblings, and do they know about me?
3. Does your side of the family know about me? How do they feel about me?
4. How was your childhood?
5. How would you describe your personality as a teen?
6. What were some of the values in your family?
7. How would you describe your parents?

95

8. What was your relationship with your parents?
9. How would you describe your grandparents?
10. What are some family traditions that you had?
11. How did you celebrate birthdays and holidays?
12. Are you married, and how did you meet the person?
13. What is your educational background, and what do you do as a career?
14. Do you have any worthy friendships?
15. How did you get through difficult times in your life?
16. Who was your role model?
17. What type of trouble did you use to get into?
18. What were the best moments of your life?
19. What are your hobbies and interests? Favorite activities to do?
20. What is your favorite Sports team or television show?
21. What is your belief system?
22. What is the next step for us?

Common Interests

Try to discover common interests that you share to find ways to bond with each other. I learned that not only was ginger ale our favorite drink, but my father and I shared a common interest in our careers. It was easy to talk to him about working with at-risk youth. We had our spirituality in common. As I stated previously, he is responsible for leading me to Christ. I was interested in having these discussions since my salvation meant a lot to him, and he helped me understand the significance. You may be surprised about what you and your father have in common that you can discuss.

Bonding Activities

But suppose, although unlikely, you do not have one thing in common. You can develop new common interests and do these things together. Maybe your father is into something t you wouldn't mind getting into. Or perhaps you have personal interests that you think he would enjoy. You are just trying to find ways to bond. For example, maybe there is a television series you recommend he watch or vice versa. It can be something you both will be doing and then come together and discuss. It can be playing board games or doing puzzles together. Other activities may include attending sports events, going out to eat (the restaurant doesn't have to be fancy, you can go to a fast-food restaurant), taking a trip together, and going camping. If you have a family of your own, you can invite your father over for dinner and include him in any family activities, outings, or gatherings.

The important thing is that you are spending time together. Be open to learning from each other. Allow your father to teach you new things. As mentioned in the "My Reunion" chapter, I remember when my father and his wife came to California to visit me for a week. We had a great time. I showed them around California as he had never been here before. We went to Universal Studios, Venice Beach, the mountains, Hollywood, the Queen Mary, and many other places. We were able to share these moments. As I said earlier, he even taught me some driving tips like parallel parking, something I wasn't skillful at the time. It was a father-daughter moment I won't forget.

Below are suggestions for ways to communicate with your father during relationship building.

Letter Writing

Some would perceive this form of communication as archaic. Based on my personal experience, however, it is priceless. As previously mentioned, I recommend this as the initial form of communication, at least until you feel comfortable meeting in person. As my father stated in his first letter, letter writing eliminates impromptu words. It allows you to be thoughtful in your written expression since you can take as long as you want to come up with the perfect words to reflect what you want to say to your father. Make sure to discuss letter writing with him so you can agree to be committed to writing each other back. Thus, whoever receives the first letter will be prompted to write back.

What I like about letters is the thoughtfulness and the anticipation of waiting for them. After a few days, you look for a letter and go to the mailbox, hoping it is there. It is comparable to waiting for something you ordered online.

The other thing I love about letter writing is that your father immortalized his thoughts on paper, and you can have them forever. In my case, I still have all of the letters my father wrote to me in a keepsake box, and those letters are invaluable to me now because he passed away five years into our relationship building. Now over twenty years after his death, if I want to feel close to him or am missing him, all I have to do is go into my keepsake box and reminisce by reading his letters. The experience allows me to feel like he is speaking to me. You have read examples of his letters to me in the previous chapters and throughout this book.

Email

Email is another way you can communicate with your father. If you communicate through email, read your emails regularly, as emails are not as instant as social media. Also, similar to letter writing—but not as convenient since you would have to put some effort into searching for them unless you print them out—you have the written words you can refer back to. Another similarity is that you can respond in your own time and at your own pace.

Social Media

This form of communication allows you to have continuous contact throughout the day and is beneficial for relationship building. You have your choice of options here, including text messaging, Snapchat (https:snapchat.com) Facebook Messenger (https://facebook.com), and sending direct messages through Twitter (https:twitter.com), Instagram (https://instagram.com), and others. You and your father will need to stay on top of this form of communication since it is instant.

Social media allows you to post pictures, and you can show your father photos of significant moments that he missed out on in your life. You can also keep your father up to date on current moments since meeting him.

Also, similar to letter writing—but not as convenient since you would have to put some effort into searching for the posts (if they're still available)—you have the written words you can refer back to. Another similarity is that you can respond in your own time and at your own pace. The difference is that with social media, there are those impromptu words, incomplete sentences, shorthand, text speech in acronyms, and sometimes, the use of only emojis. This type of communication is not usually as thoughtful as people are more impulsive when writing on social media. Keep in mind that your father is from a different generation. Depending on his age, he may not be as savvy at social media as you are. He may prefer good ole' phone calls.

Video Phone Calls

This form of communication allows you to have a conversation while seeing your father through video. Some apps include Skype (https:skype.com), Facebook Messenger (https://www.Facebook.com/), Google Duo (https://duo. google.com/), WhatsApp (https://whatsapp.com), Amazon Alexa (https://w ww.amazon.com/smart-home-devices/), and Zoom (https://zoom.us/). Facetime (https://apps.apple.com/us/app/facetime/) is exclusive to Apple iPhones and iPads. There are plenty of video chat apps, but these are just a few. These apps are easy to use on your mobile devices. This method is especially beneficial if this is a long-distance relationship, as was my case.

Unfortunately, video calls did not exist in the 1990s during my reunion with my father. He lived in Cleveland, Ohio, while I lived across the country in California. I wished this form of communication was available when I was building my relationship. I would have loved to have been able to see him on the calls and show him my family and things from my home. We did, however, snail mail VHS recordings to each other.

There are times when you may not feel like being seen. You may not be dressed, or have your hair combed, etc., but as you become more comfortable with each other, your appearance won't matter as much anymore.

Regular Phone Calls

I would recommend having occasional telephone contact if you mainly plan on using texting and social media as your primary mode of communication. Make sure you answer your cell phone and check your messages regularly to ensure that your voicemail box is not full. Receiving a phone call and hearing someone's voice can be a pleasant surprise. You can get the same effect with receiving a text message, but the difference here is that it is nice to hear a live voice from time to time. Nowadays, depending on the generation, you may prefer texting. As I said earlier, your father may prefer this mode of communication if he is not savvy enough in using texting and social media. He may be open to the opportunity for you to teach him. You should also be open to phone calls as the primary form of communication if this is the only way he wants to have contact.

In-Person Visits

If you can see him often, great! But the likelihood is that you may only be able to see him occasionally. The previously mentioned forms of communication are building blocks for laying the foundation of the relationship. They are non-threatening, less awkward, and convenient ways to help you learn more about each other and help you become more comfortable when you have in-person contact. At least if you have been communicating consistently, this will increase your comfort level when interacting in person. I found in my experience that it felt natural whenever I was in his presence, even when I met him for the first time.

Building Relationships With Paternal Relatives

Connecting, not just with your father but also with your paternal relatives, is beneficial. A lot of your conversations can relate to gaining information about your newly found family. Hopefully, your father has a positive relationship with his side of the family or at least some people he can connect to you. Then you can engage with them through social media and build your relationship with them.

Don't be surprised if paternal relatives are not willing to accept you. They may have their hang-ups regarding the situation. Perhaps, they have an issue with your mother or have something personal against her. Although it may be hurtful, try not to take it personally. In my case, I discovered there are a lot of relatives on my father's side. I found out when I attended my first family reunion in 2016 for his maternal side of the family in Los Angeles, CA.

My Experience with Paternal Relatives

I was overwhelmed by the number of relatives on my father's side of the family. Over the years, I have only maintained a relationship with my sister and her immediate family, paternal grandfather, brothers, and a cousin who has always kept me in the loop.

My grandfather, who is now deceased, reached out to me shortly after my father passed away. I was pleasantly surprised to hear from him as we were both still in mourning. I felt like I now had a new connection to my father, even after his passing. I knew I could learn more about my father from my paternal grandfather since he raised him. I saw him as an extension of my father. It was like I was maintaining my connection with my father through him. I saw him as a wealth of information to continue learning more about my father and myself.

My grandfather wrote me a letter educating me about his own life. It included his retirement party video, copies of his retirement papers, and photos of him and my father. Receiving the letter from him was reminiscent of when my father sent me letters. My grandfather also sent me a Christmas card every year, and I kept everything that he and my father sent to me in the keepsake box (that I mentioned earlier in the letter-writing section). He even met my three children once when I was visiting Cleveland, and he took us to a movie and then to eat at Bob Evans. We called each other on the phone occasionally, and we maintained our relationship for over thirteen years until he passed away in 2017.

I did not have a relationship with my paternal grandmother, although I wished I did. On the day of my father's funeral, she did not acknowledge me. At that moment, I assumed she did not want anything to do with me. For years, I had it in my mind that she did not like me or did not want to accept me. Over the years, I desired to call her to try and start a relationship with her. She was my grandmother, after all.

When I went to Cleveland in November 2016 to spend time with my maternal grandparents, my paternal sister helped me see things differently. She said that she may have been that way towards me because of her feelings on the day of her son's funeral, and it was nothing personal against me. I had not even considered that before. As my sister told me this, we were traveling in her car, and she asked if I wanted her to take me to my paternal grandmother's home to visit her. I was willing to take that chance as I was curious whether she would accept me or not.

Here was the moment of truth. So when we arrived, surprisingly, my grandmother treated me as if she had known me and loved me all this time. It was a pleasant visit. I was so glad my sister convinced me to go over there—it was a life-changing moment. Do you mean I was feeling this way all these years for nothing?

Due to my assumption, I missed out on developing a relationship with my grandmother. Even though she did not reach out to me as my paternal grandfather did, I could have reached out to her. Now, I will not have the opportunity. I believe it was God's will for me to go to Cleveland at the time. It was the first and last time I would spend time with my paternal grandmother. It was also my last time seeing my paternal grandfather, as they both passed away a few months after this visit.

So although that visit was originally intended for me to visit my ailing grandfather on my mother's side, the Lord had a purpose. He planned for me to make peace with my situation regarding my paternal grandmother and to see both paternal grandparents for the last time. As a result of assuming my grandmother wanted nothing to do with me, I missed out on an opportunity to have a relationship with her. Please do not make the same mistake of basing your relative's initial reaction to you on whether or not they accept you. Learn more about the reasons before writing them off in your mind. I carried around unnecessary pain when all I had to do was take a risk and reach out to her. The Lord always has a way of working situations out.

My paternal sister and I and our families continue to maintain a relationship. I am so blessed to have her and her family in my life, even if she is one of the few connections I have to my paternal side of the family. I don't maintain as much contact with my brothers. However, I keep abreast of their lives through social media and visit them whenever I am in Cleveland. There was a time, several years ago, when one of my brothers came out to California, and while he was here, he spent time with my family at Venice Beach. It was fun with him as I got to know him better and learned a little more about my father.

I am thankful for my paternal cousin, that has kept in touch with me over the years. She and my father were close. They were like brothers and sisters. Since I met my father, she has been involved in my life by consistently keeping me informed of everything in the family. For example, she emails the entire family a family newsletter that keeps everyone current on any important news, including ill family members needing prayer, death announcements, birthdays, graduations, upcoming family reunions, and family history information. She is the one that keeps everyone connected on my father's maternal side of the family, and I appreciate her for this.

So you can't just stop at the initial reunion. You must continue and make an effort to build a positive relationship with your father. I have discussed some essential components of building a positive relationship with your father and provided the methods to assist you with this task. Whichever type of communication you use, be consistent and ultimately have an in-person contact at some point. What should you do if it doesn't work out?

15

Better off Apart and How to Deal with the Loss

Unfortunately, not everyone will have a fairy tale ending. Maybe you utilized the resources in the "Be Your Own Investigator" chapter, but you still did not find your father. Or perhaps you found out he passed away several years ago. Or maybe you successfully located him and attempted to make initial contact, but he never responded. Or he did respond, but not in the way you had hoped he would; he was indifferent or appeared uninterested in meeting you or seeing you again. These are just a few reasons why the reunion didn't work out. The question is, now what? Where do you go from here?

It is crucial to realize that you have already begun to heal through the processes outlined in this book. You went through understanding and acknowledging the void in your life due to your father's absence. You also began to understand your emotions, process your feelings and identify your needs. You learned to forgive through letter-writing, recognizing and transforming your distorted thoughts. If you end up not having a relationship, try to be at peace with it. The fact is that you did all that you possibly could do within your ability to have a relationship.

Radical Acceptance

According to Marsha Linehan, founder of Dialectical Behavioral Therapy, "Radical acceptance rests on letting go of the illusion of control and a willingness to notice and accept things as they are right now, without judging." Allow reality to be as it is. A loss will always be difficult and painful, but acceptance means you can begin to heal. So if your attempt at reuniting with your father did not work out as you had hoped it would, then instead of being devastated, just tell yourself, "It is what it is." Some sample radical acceptance responses include:

"I couldn't find him, and I am disappointed about this, but it is what it is; I can't change this outcome."

"I found him, but he rejected me. It sucks, and I am not OK with it, but it is what it is; I cannot change how he feels."

"I found out that he passed away, and I feel bad that I never got to meet him, but it is what it is; I cannot change this outcome."

Unfortunately, you cannot avoid the pain, but you have control over how much you want to suffer this pain. Radical acceptance will reduce the amount of suffering time. As long as you've tried everything to have a positive outcome, radical acceptance will come easier.

Remember Forgiveness

Try to avoid those negative feelings you once had, as having a negative experience can set you back. Instead, reflect on the previous exercise in Chapter eleven where you wrote a forgiveness letter. Remember, if you have successfully completed that exercise, you have already forgiven your father for not being a part of your life. Have an open mind and give him the benefit of the doubt.

No Regrets

If you have made the most out of the information in this book, found it helpful, and completed all the exercises, then you have taken charge of your healing. At this point, have no regrets because you are likely better off today after going through your healing journey than if you did not read this book. You will only get out of this book what you put into it. In this case, you had to put yourself into this process to get results.

Ending On Good Terms

Try, if possible, to end on good terms with your father. It will depend on you and how you react to the situation. If, for example, you are unsuccessful in your multiple attempts to contact your father, leave a positive voicemail message or text message, or write a final letter saying:

> *"I wished that this could have worked out. If you ever want to contact me, you have my information. Hope to hear from you soon."*

Suppose you successfully contact him (i.e., a telephone call, in-person), and it appears that he shows no interest in having a relationship with you or may not be ready to have one due to his current circumstances. You can say the above directly to him and let him know whenever he is ready you will be there. It leaves the door open and lets your father know that you have no resentment or ill feelings toward him.

You never know what the circumstances may be. Perhaps your initiating contact may have triggered guilt and shame about being absent in the first place, so he may not be ready to face you. Your father may also be battling "demons" in the sense of substance use, among others, and doesn't want you to see him in that condition. So instead of assuming it has to do with you (personalization), it may have to do with him. So let him know the door is open whenever he is ready. Try not to fixate on whether or not he will contact you. Instead, think in your mind:

"I tried, and if he contacts me, great. If he never does, I know I did all that I could."

This way, you will have closure.

Gratitude

Even though it didn't work out with your father, it is helpful to recognize the positive things you have in your life. Numerous studies demonstrate that gratitude journaling, for example, increases happiness.

Self-Love

It is important to realize that regardless of having a relationship with your father or not, you must love yourself. Not knowing who your father is or feeling rejected by him should not negate your self-worth. If you struggle in this area 'Recognize Your Strengths' exercise below can increase your personal awareness.

Closure Steps

I recommend five steps to attain closure with your father. Take as much time as you need to work through each step of this process.

Closure Step #1- Final Contact

As mentioned in the "Ending On Good Terms" section, make one last contact using any form of communication of your choosing. I would recommend writing a letter if you have the address, as this allows you to be thoughtful in how you want to give your final expression.

Closure Step #2- Acceptance Journal or Letter

After making that last contact with your final expressions, I recommend journaling. Once you have accepted it is what it is (radical acceptance), you may experience disappointment, anger, or sadness about not being reunited with your father. This reaction is normal. Journaling can be an effective way to identify and process your feelings. It is a way to release and dump them into the book instead of keeping them bottled up inside you.

A second option, if you decided not to do step #1, is to write a letter as if you are going to give it to your father, expressing that you have accepted the situation for what it is.

Closure Step #3- Gratitude Exercise

Even though it didn't work out with your father, it is helpful to recognize the positive things you have in your life. Try to write down all the people and things you appreciate. You can make it a daily practice to do gratitude journaling.

Closure Step #4- Recognize Your Strengths and Accomplishments Exercise

Make a list of your positive qualities and strengths that you believe you have to reinforce your resilience and sense of self despite your absent father issues. Then make a list of all of your accomplishments. You can even create affirmation cards out of these strengths and reflect on them daily, or write them on post-it notes and stick them on your wall, refrigerator, or mirror.

Closure Step #5- Support Buddy Contact

I encourage you to reach out to your support buddy and review your journey. Discuss the process and how it has helped you, as well as the steps of closure so they can support you in your continued healing. After all, they were on this journey with you throughout the entire process. Also, their support does not have to end when this book ends. Keep them involved, as you may experience residual feelings after reading this book.

Seeking Professional Help

If you continue to struggle emotionally after this process, I recommend seeking professional support. This support can include individual therapy, support groups, or counseling with your clergy (based on your religious affiliation) so you can further process your experience.

The next chapter will discuss identifying others in your life to who you can turn.

16

A Suitable Surrogate for Your Life

What does it mean to have a suitable surrogate? A surrogate, by definition, is a substitute. Was there a substitute father in your life? A male figure who fulfilled the paternal role in the absence of your father? If there wasn't any while growing up, is there an individual who can fulfill this role now? I believe a person is never too old to have a suitable surrogate. Below are some examples. It is important to note that you can have more than one type of suitable surrogate, and they all can complement each other in terms of fulfilling your needs.

Having a suitable surrogate can play a role in one's healthy development. I want you to reflect on your own life. Was there someone in your life who was a suitable surrogate? Had a positive impact on your development? You may not have realized the impact on your life, but you can feel good that you had someone to stand in the gap left by your absent father. Of course, there is no ideal replacement for a biological father as you can only have one of those due to DNA, but there are some close seconds.

Fortunately, I was never without a suitable surrogate. I attribute my healthy development and upbringing to having these suitable surrogates. At this point in your life, try to identify any needs you wish your father could have met that a suitable surrogate can help you with. If appropriate, refe to the letter in Chapter eight, "What I Need From My Father." You may continue to need emotional support, guidance on relationships, career, how to do tasks that a father would typically teach his child, etc. Whatever your individual need is, advocate for yourself to get it met.

Grandfathers

Of course, both grandparents can play a significant role in your life. For the sake of this book, I am focusing on the male figure—the grandfather. Grandfathers can stand in the gap for your biological father, making them suitable surrogates. I have noticed multiple children placed with their grandparents throughout my career working in foster care. It also happens with children not even in the foster care system.

My very first suitable surrogate was my grandfather. He was affectionately referred to as "Andad" because the oldest cousin could not say "granddad" while he was little, so this name just stuck. Andad was in my life since birth because my mom and I lived with my grandparents in Cleveland, Ohio. I didn't even miss having my biological father at the time because Andad was there for me. We enjoyed spending quality time together as he let me tag along all the time and even let me ride on the back of his motorcycle. When I was little, I always wanted to be around him. He horse-played with me, took me to the cabin in Pennsylvania during the summers, bought me train sets, gave me tons of advice about cars and driving, etc. The list goes on.

Unfortunately, he passed away, but I know he is with the Lord. Even to this day, he continues to have an impact on me. If your grandfather is still living, try to form a stronger bond if you haven't already. Try to learn all you can from him.

Stepfathers

My mother became married, and we moved to California. Then I had another suitable surrogate—my stepfather. He has been in my life since I was five years old until the present. Unfortunately, stepfathers get a bad rap because of how the media portrays them and the numerous cases of sexual abuse perpetrated by stepfathers. Not all stepfathers are perverts.

My stepfather, who continues to be in my life until this day, was and continues to be a great father figure. He has loved me and treated me like his biological daughter throughout my life. He gave me a healthy childhood and supported me in many ways. He especially did when it came to academics. He was the reason I attended UCLA, my dream school. I don't see him as anything other than my father. Even after my biological father came into my life, this didn't change my relationship with my stepfather. I saw myself as now having two fathers.

If you were fortunate to have a good stepfather like me, appreciate that relationship and the fact that he stood in the gap for your biological father. Not everyone has a positive stepfather figure. If you had one, consider yourself blessed.

Uncles and Other Male Relatives

You may have male family members that have been instrumental in your upbringing. Perhaps they invited you to go on outings with them, or maybe they taught you how to drive and was a protector, or even a provider. As mentioned above about grandparents, multiple children in foster care live with their aunts and uncles. They took in their nieces and nephews when their biological parents couldn't care for their children. So the uncle was their suitable surrogate.

It was the case in one of my favorite sitcoms, "The Bernie Mac Show." Bernie Mac raises his nieces and nephew because his sister is a drug addict and unable to care for her children. This sitcom was based on his real-life story. It happens in real life more than you realize. There may be other adults, biological or non-biological male relatives, like cousins, older brothers, etc., who may have fulfilled this role.

Even as an adult, if these family members are still available, it is never too late to utilize them as suitable surrogates. See who you have a bond with and try to strengthen that bond. As I said, it is never too late.

Church Members/Clergy

Depending on your religion, your pastor, priest, rabbi, etc., may help your moral development. They can also provide you with emotional support and help you with your decision-making skills. Also, they have to ensure confidentiality so you can confide in them.

Mentors

Maybe there was someone in your life who didn't fit into any of the above categories, but they had an impact on you. You may have seen them as a mentor, someone who provided guidance for you. It is never too late to have a mentor in your life. You can seek out a mentor for yourself at this point if you believe you are still in need of guidance in a particular area in your life. For example, you may feel you need someone to advise you regarding your career or relationships. It can be a male figure you grew up knowing or even recently met, like a neighbor, family friend, church member, etc.

In the following chapter, I will be introducing to some of you and reacquainting or confirming for others the ultimate, perfect suitable surrogate—My Heavenly Father.

17

Seeking the Ultimate Father

As mentioned at the beginning of this book, I am a Christian. In Chapter thirteen, "My Reunion Story", you read about how my biological father was instrumental in my becoming a Christian. I believed this was the best decision that I have made in my entire life, and that it was providential that my father came into my life at the time he did. If it were not for God, I would not have met my father and had my fatherless void healed, and enjoyed the profoundly impactful five-year relationship I had with him.

If you are reading this book for your well-being, you still need something to fill that void. I would be remiss if I did not share the joys of having God as a Father. Even if I didn't have any father figure in my life, I am confident that God could fill the void. Likewise, whether or not you have a father figure, God can be the ultimate Father, greater than any earthly father you could ever have.

For this reason, this chapter is devoted to God as the Ultimate Father. I know Him personally, and you can too. Following are some of His primary qualities as a father figure that I've discovered over time. I know the God of the Bible, to be loving, a disciplinarian, a role model, a provider, a protector, fair, compassionate, a teacher, a promise keeper, patient, and forgiving. I can speak from personal experience that God has been all of those things and more.

God as a Father

Let us look at the traits of both our ideal earthly father and our Heavenly Father. These traits help us understand who the God of the Bible is. In fact, He is a perfect father figure who can fulfill all of our needs.

- Loves unconditionally
- Disciplinarian
- Role Model
- Provider
- Protector
- Moral
- Compassionate
- Teacher
- Promise Keeper
- Patient
- Forgiving

Loving

For God so loved the world that he gave his one and only Son, that whoever believes in him should not perish but have eternal life (John 3:16 New International Version, 1973/2011).

Above all else, God is the epitome of love. Just like any ideal earthly father, God delights in generously pouring out His love onto his children. In His role as our Heavenly Father, the scope of God's love goes way beyond even the most loving earthly fathers. God's love is unfailing, generous, abundant, and unconditional. His love is everlasting. The greatest act of love that God has shown the world is allowing His only Son to die for our sins as a ransom sacrifice, so we do not have to endure the punishment we deserve. He even demonstrated that He had conquered death by raising that Son up from His grave three days later. No earthly father is even capable of the type of love our Heavenly father displays on a daily basis to His children.

Disciplinarian

And have you completely forgotten this word of encouragement that addresses you as a father addresses his son? It says, "My son, do not make light of the Lord's discipline, and do not lose heart when he rebukes you, because the Lord disciplines the one he loves, and he chastens everyone he accepts as his son." Endure hardship as discipline; God is treating you as his children. For what children are not disciplined by their father? (New International Version, 1973/2011, Hebrews 12:5-7).

God's knowledge of our individual situations, coupled with His unparalleled wisdom, enables Him to deal perfectly with us every time, bringing about the good in us and for us. The earthly father's role is often to be a disciplinarian, but he may not always know the best way to deal with his child. He may even be overbearing and/or lacking wisdom. God uses the situations in our lives to correct us and straighten our paths.

Role Model

"Follow God's example, therefore, as dearly loved children" (New International Version, 1973/2011, Ephesians 5:1).

Earthly fathers should be positive role models to their children. They should demonstrate qualities that are worth imitating. They should be honest, upright, have morals, and walk with integrity. Our Heavenly Father is perfect in all of these areas. He is holy and unequivocally righteous. We will never be perfect, but we should strive to have the qualities of our Heavenly Father, for He gives us the blueprint (in the bible) to live a righteous life.

Provider

"Therefore I tell you, do not worry about your life, what you will eat or drink; or about your body, what you will wear. Is not life more than food, and the body more than clothes? Look at the birds of the air; they do not sow or reap or store away in barns, and yet your heavenly Father feeds them. Are you not much more valuable than they?" (New International Version, 1973/2011, Matthew 6:25-26).

One of an earthly father's roles is to provide for his family financially. Our Heavenly Father also provides for us. Since He is all-knowing and omnipresent, He is always aware of our needs. God knows our physical, financial, and emotional needs, and can provide beyond what any earthly father is capable of providing. He provides for the needs of His children right on time.

Protector

Whoever dwells in the shelter of the Most High will rest in the shadow of the Almighty. I will say of the Lord, "He is my refuge and my fortress, my God, in whom I trust. Surely He will save you from the fowler's snare and from the deadly pestilence. He will cover you with his feathers, and under his wings you will find refuge; his faithfulness will be your shield and rampart (New International Version, 1973/2011, Psalm 91:1-4).

When you have God in your life, you can call on Him at any time through the mechanism of prayer. Prayer is our way of effectively communicating with our Heavenly Father. God hears our prayers during our times of trouble, and He will respond to our earnest needs and provide security. I have been a witness to His ability to rescue His children even during the most difficult of situations, so many times.

Moral

Let no debt remain outstanding, except the continuing debt to love one another, for whoever loves others has fulfilled the law. The commandments, "You shall not commit adultery," "You shall not murder," "You shall not steal," "You shall not covet," and whatever other command there may be, are summed up in this one command: "Love your neighbor as yourself." Love does no harm to a neighbor. Therefore love is the fulfillment of the law (New International Version, 1973/2011, Romans 13:8-10).

Moral means being concerned with right and wrong behavior. A child will look to his earthly father for an example of how to behave in society. The ideal earthly father should be modeling appropriate conduct for his children. Our Heavenly Father also has rules for us to live by that ensure that our behavior is in line with the laws of the land today. The Bible reveals that the greatest commandment is to love one another. This ensures that we treat others with respect if we want them to treat us the same way. God sees all we do; even the things we hide away from others or that we secretly think. He informs us what is right and wrong through His word and within our own consciences, and He metes out appropriate consequences when we do not comply. But He tempers those consequences with mercy. And because He allowed His Son to die on the cross for our sins, those who accept Him will never have to experience the ultimate consequence.

Compassionate

Praise be to the God and Father of our Lord Jesus Christ, the Father of compassion and the God of all comfort, who comforts us in all our troubles, so that we can comfort those in any trouble with the comfort we ourselves receive from God (New International Version, 1973/2011, 2 Corinthians 1:3-4).

"Can a mother forget the baby at her breast and have no compassion for the child she has borne? Though she may forget, I will not forget you!" (New International Version, 1973/2011, Isaiah 49:15).

When a child is hurting for whatever reason, a good earthly father feels compassion for that child and deals with their physical, mental, and/or emotional pain in comforting ways. God, our Heavenly Father has promised never to leave us nor forsake us. His attentiveness to our needs and devotion to fulfilling them will not end. There is a tremendous amount of comfort in knowing that God is aware of the struggles we go through and is willing to help us through them.

Teacher

All Scripture is God-breathed and is useful for teaching, rebuking, correcting and training in righteousness, so that the servant of God may be thoroughly equipped for every good work (New International Version, 1973/2011, 2 Timothy 3:16-17).

The earthly father teaches his child everything from throwing a football and how to do a math problem, to dealing with life's most challenging moments. My Heavenly Father includes everything you need to know to live a righteous and spiritually prosperous life in the Bible. For example, His Word teaches you how to treat and help others, have a successful marriage, raise your children, and how to build your character. The Bible is supernaturally designed to be a resource in one's life. Scriptures may be read many times, but as we grow and mature, the same scriptures can shed new light on our current situation. God also teaches us through life lessons and the wisdom he imparts to others.

Promise Keeper

"Know therefore that the Lord your God is God; he is the faithful God, keeping his covenant of love to a thousand generations of those who love him and keep his commandments" (New International Version, 1973/2011, Deuteronomy 7:9).

An earthly father sometimes makes promises to his children without the ability to keep them. For example, a father may promise his child that he will take him or her somewhere or buy him something and not follow through. God made promises to His earthly children throughout the Bible, and He has been faithful in keeping them forever. God is incapable of lying, so, therefore, He's incapable of breaking His promises.

Patient

"The Lord is gracious and compassionate, slow to anger and rich in love" (New International Version, 1973/2011, Psalm 145:8).

Sometimes a child can try the patience of their parents when the child is being disobedient and stubborn, which results in the parents becoming frustrated. My Heavenly Father, however, is merciful and slow to anger. He allows us to mess up over and over again until we learn to follow His ways. He never makes rash decisions, but lovingly waits until we're able to see a situation from His perspective and make the necessary course of corrections based on His word.

Forgiving

For I will forgive their wickedness and will remember their sins no more (New International Version, 1973/2011, Romans 8:12).

Finally, when we mess up more times than not, our parents will forgive us. But sometimes, their forgiveness will only go so far. There are times when a child can do something so heinous or so in the parent's eye, which will even make that parent not forgive them. When we sincerely ask God for forgiveness and make a promise within ourselves not to repeat the offense, it is known as repentance. When God encounters a truly repentant heart, he wipes the slate clean and remembers the offense no more.

There are so many things we do and don't do that miss the mark of God's holy standard. And yet, he forgives us daily. In the same way, if God can forgive us, He asks that we forgive others; like our absent fathers. The exercises in Chapter eleven, "I Forgive You Letter," were designed to help you be more like God in a way; you are able to embrace the forgiveness of your earthly father and others.

Everlasting

"Do you not know Have you not heard? The Lord is the everlasting God, the Creator of the ends of the earth. He will not grow tired or weary, and his understanding no one can fathom" (New International Version, 1973/2011, Isaiah 40:28).

Finally, there is one quality that our Heavenly Father has that no earthly father possesses or can ever be to a child; He is everlasting. God is our Everlasting Father. Even the ideal earthly father cannot be available 24/7 due to work and other responsibilities or physical limitations. God, on the other hand, is always with us, always available, and will never die or go away. In fact, one of God's most profound promises is that He will "...never leave you, nor forsake you..". It's an awesome feeling to know that God our Heavenly Father, the Creator of the Universe, loves each one of us individually and has our backs every single day of our lives.

If you know God personally as I do, I encourage you to see God as your Father who can stand in the gap in the areas your earthly father falls short, or replace your earthly father completely if he is not in your life at all or has passed on. If you had a relationship with God at one time and then went astray, I am encouraging you to return to God and restore your relationship with Him. The parable of the Prodigal Son in the Bible reinforces the idea that God will rejoice if you return to Him. The key, of course, to knowing God as your Father and having a personal relationship with Him, is to first believe in Him and believe that the Bible is His word for us. Do you desire to have Him in your life so He can be the perfect Father to you and fulfill your needs? It's exciting to share the steps below to become a Christian because of the blessings that are sure to follow. Once we accept God as our Father and become adopted into His family, we inherit all the riches he has stored up for us in Heaven.

Steps to Becoming a Christian

First of all, it is important to realize that every human being has sinned or committed wrongdoings and has fallen short of the glory of God (New International Version, 1973/2011, Romans 3:23). Secondly, it is essential to understand that we cannot save ourselves. Salvation is not something we deserve or can earn. Thirdly, the Gospel Message in the Bible reveals that because of God's perfect holiness, grace, mercy, and abundant love for mankind, He wanted to provide a way to bring us back into the right relationship with him. That solution for us is known as the plan of salvation. In order to become a Christian, you must follow the steps outlined below:

1. Admit that you are a sinner.

For the wages of sin is death, but the gift of God is eternal life in Christ Jesus our Lord (New International Version, 1973/2011, Romans 6:23).

Sin entered the world with the first man and woman, Adam and Eve, and their disobedience to God. They were created to live forever in the Garden of Eden, but because of their disobedient act—they and through them—all mankind would suffer the consequences of being separated from God and having a limited lifespan, eternally separated from God. Our sin makes us accountable to God and worthy of eternal punishment because we have sinned against a Holy and Eternal God. In order to become a Christian, believe and admit to making mistakes and that you're a sinner; ask for God's forgiveness, and then turn away from sinning willfully —as mentioned earlier, that is called repentance.

2. Believe that God sent His Son.

For God so loved the world that he gave his one and only Son, that whoever believes in him shall not perish but have eternal life (New International Version, 1973/2011, John 3:16).

Jesus Christ died on the cross for our sins. Without this loving act, we had no hope because sin is a death sentence. Because of God's love for us, He initiated His eternal plan to save us. God the Father sent his only Son to be born as a man and live a perfect life so that He could be qualified to die in our place. Jesus died for our sins. Three days later, Jesus was raised from the dead, proving God's power over death. To reap the benefits of that sacrifice, we must believe that Jesus is God's Son and that He died for our sins and rose from the grave on the third day.

3. Confess

If you declare with your mouth, "Jesus is Lord," and believe in your heart that God raised him from the dead, you will be saved. For it is with your heart that you believe and are justified, and it is with your mouth that you profess your faith and are saved (New International Version, 1973/2011, Romans 10:9-10).

Lastly, it is essential that you accept Jesus Christ as your Lord and Savior, and rely on Him alone by faith, for your salvation. You need to commit yourself to a life of following Jesus and serving others. If you understand and believe in everything that was stated above, and have accepted Jesus as your personal Savior you can say this prayer below:

> *Dear God,*
>
> *I know I have sinned and missed the mark as established in your word. I humbly ask for your forgiveness. I believe Jesus Christ is Your Son. I believe that He gave His perfect life for my sins and that you raised Him to life after three days. I want to surrender to Him as my Savior and follow Him as Lord, from this day forward. Please guide my life and help me to do Your will. Furthermore, I petition You to adopt me into Your Holy Family and Become my Heavenly Father whom I can praise and call upon at all times. I pray this in the name of Jesus my Redeemer. Amen.*

Now, let someone know about this important life-changing step you just took in becoming a Christian.

18

Post-Self-Emotional Assessment

Now that you have come to the end of the book, let's debrief the entire experience.

Were you able to identify a support system to help you through the process? Was your support buddy helpful? If so, in what ways?

Describe how you were able to identify, confront, and process your feelings about your absent father's issues.

Describe how you effectively utilized the AFERA tool in helping you deal with your emotions. Please explain if you did not.

Are there any medical/ mental health conditions that you are curious about that may run on your father's side of the family? How do you plan to look into it further?

Do you now have a better understanding of your mom's role in the situation?

Were you able to identify what you need from your father? If you can reunite with him, do you plan to discuss these needs with him?

Please discuss if you were able to identify your negative core beliefs, and transform your negative thoughts.

Did you forgive your father? If so, please discuss how that process was for you. If not, please discuss what the barrier to forgiveness is.

Did you take a risk, or are you willing to seek him out with the assistance of the "Be Your Own Investigator" chapter? If you found your father, please discuss how that process was for you.

If you successfully reunited with your father, or intend to reunite with your father how do you plan to build a positive and lasting relationship with him?

If the reunion did not work out, or you decided not to reunite with him, did you learn radical acceptance to deal with the loss and move on?

AFERA Post-Test

Only the resentment and regret sections are included in the post-test to determine if these negative emotions have improved. Add the total number of yes answers out of 20. Each yes is worth 5 points. Compare your original score from the initial self-assessment that you completed at the beginning of the book and see if your scores improved.

Resentment

I resent my father for the following (please circle yes or no):
1. For abandoning me and not being a part of my life. Yes No
2. For not caring enough about me to have me in his life. Yes No
3. For not showing me love. Yes No
4. For having another family. Yes No
5. For the way he treated my mom. Yes No
6. For the way he treated me. Yes No
7. For my insecurities. Yes No
8. For my deep-rooted anger. Yes No
9. For not supporting me financially. Yes No
10. For all the troubles I got into in my younger years. Yes No
11. For my lack of proper upbringing. Yes No
12. For my emotional problems. Yes No
13. For my relationship problems. Yes No

14. For my academic problems. Yes No

15. For not being available to talk to. Yes No

16. For making me feel rejected. Yes No

17. For my substance use problems or other self-destructive habits. Yes No

18. For my self-esteem issues. Yes No

19. For my distrust of others. Yes No

20. For not being a positive male role model in my life. Yes No

Initial score–

Post-test score–

Regret

I have regrets because of my father not doing the following and for depriving me of some of these things (please circle yes or no):

1. I feel like I missed out on having a father. Yes No

2. I regret not knowing about the other part of me. Yes No

3. I wish he could have been there for the important events in my life. Yes No

4. For not being the head of my family. Yes No

5. For not being there for my school events. Yes No

6. For not providing for me financially. Yes No

7. For not helping me with making important life decisions. Yes No

8. For not having him as a protector. Yes No

9. For him not seeing me grow up. Yes No

10. For not having him in the same home. Yes No

11. For not seeing my mom loved by a good man. Yes No

12. For missing my birthdays. Yes No

13. For not celebrating the holidays with me. Yes No

14. For not attending my graduation(s). Yes No

15. For not attending my sports events. Yes No

16. For not helping me with relationships. Yes No

17. For not spending quality time with me. Yes No

18. For not being there to talk about my problems. Yes No

19. For not being there to be a role model. Yes No

20. For not being my disciplinarian. Yes No

Initial score–

Post-test score–

Remember, scoring 60 points or higher in either section indicates the need to work on that area. Did that score go down? If so, congratulations on successfully working on your healing. If the score did not improve, ask yourself the following questions:

- What was my mindset when I first started reading this book?
- Did I approach my healing journey with an open mind?
- Did I take full advantage of the information and exercises in this book?

How would you rate the intensity level of your resentment on a scale of 1–10 before going through this book? Ten being the most intense. Please circle your response.

1 2 3 4 5 6 7 8 9 10

How would you rate the intensity level of your resentment on a scale of 1–10 after going through this book? Please circle your response.

1 2 3 4 5 6 7 8 9 10

How would you rate the intensity level of your regretful feelings on a scale of 1–10 before going through this book? Ten being the most intense. Please circle your response.

1 2 3 4 5 6 7 8 9 10

How would you rate the intensity level of your regretful feelings on a scale of 1–10 after going through this book? Please circle your response.

1 2 3 4 5 6 7 8 9 10

If your rating decreased even a little bit in either of these two areas, then that is an improvement.

If there was still no improvement either in a decrease in score or intensity level then consider going back through the book, and redoing some of the exercises.

Outcome (circle all that apply):

1. I found my birth father. Yes No
2. I started seeking out my birth father. Yes No
3. I plan on seeking out my birth father. Yes No
4. I am working on building a relationship with my birth father. Yes No
5. I have accepted that we are better off apart. I'm coping with this. Yes No

I hope that this book has effectively helped you on your journey of self-discovery and promoted the healing of your fatherless void.

19

Breaking the Cycle of the Absent Father Syndrome

Y ou may already have a child or children or someday decide to have children. Since you knew how it felt to go through your life without your father, you should not want that experience for your children. As a female, no matter the circumstances with your child's father, you must ensure that your child's father is involved in their life. After reading this book, hopefully, you understand how the lack of father involvement affects your child's emotional, academic, and social functioning. By encouraging and maintaining father involvement, you give your child the best advantage in life because they will have the best of both worlds. They will have an opportunity to excel.

As a plea to the males reading this book, if you already have children or plan to have children, get involved if you are not already, and stay involved. You now know the effects of a father's absence. Do not subject your children to what you endured while growing up. Be there for your children. Barack Obama once said when he was talking about his father, "I came to appreciate the degree to which I wanted to be president in my children's life. That's not something he taught me directly. He taught me by his absence." At this point, if you separate from your children for whatever reason, make every effort to initiate contact using this book as a resource guide. After all, based on your personal experience, you know the journey your child will be on if you are not involved. It will become a generational cycle.

Also, be an advocate for others around you who are dealing with absent father problems. I found that people within our circle of influence, young and old, are dealing with this issue and perhaps are suffering in silence. If you know someone who may be experiencing what you did, encourage them, especially if you found healing by reading this book. Share your healing journey so they may be encouraged and empowered to heal their fatherless void. If you know of fathers not involved with their children, encourage them to do so and educate them on the effects of their absence.

As I mentioned in the preface of this book, there is an absent father crisis in America. You can make a difference by pledging to be committed to the above pleas by going to my Bring Dads Back Campaign page on Facebook (https://www.facebook.com/bringdadsback). Encourage others to pledge as well.

Together, let's do our part in ending the absent father syndrome!

References

Ackerman, C. E. (2017). *25 CBT techniques and worksheets for cognitive behavioral therapy.* Retrieved from https://positive psychology.com/ct-cognitive-behavioral-therapy-techniques- worksheets/

American Heritage Dictionary of the English Language. (n.d.). *Regret. In ahdictionary.com/word/search.* Retrieved from https://ahdictionary.com/word/search.html?q=regretsAmerican Heritage Dictionary

Brown, Lachlan. (2015). *The importance of developing curiosity.* Retrieved from https://psychcentral.com/blog/the-importance-of-developing-curiosity#1

Chung, E., Glanz, M., Adhopia, V. CBC News (2018). *Donor-conceived people are tracking down their biological fathers, even if they want to hide.* Retrieved from https://www.cbc.ca/news/science/sperm-donor-dna-testing-1.4500517

Greater Faith Grace Bible Church (n.d.) *How to be saved.* Retrieved from https://www.gfgbcrialto.org/page/how-to-be-saved

Hall, K. Ph.D. (2012). *Radical acceptance sometimes problems can't be solved.* Retrieved from https://www.psychologytoday.com/us/blog/pieces-mind/201207/radical acceptance

Holy Bible, New King James Version (1982).https://www.biblegateway.com/
versions/New-King-James-Version-NKJV-Bible/

Horesh N., Sommerfeld E., Wolf M, Zubery E., Zalsman G.(2014)
Father-daughter relationship and the severity of eating disorders. Retrieved
from https://pubmed.ncbi.nlm.nih.gov/24908149/

Keaney, T., Tenaglia, L., Zweig, S., Collins, C. Cechin-De La Rosa, C.,
& Barclay, M. (2018). *My next guest needs no introduction with David Letterman
Barack Obama as first guest* https://www.netflix.com/title/80209096

Linehan, M. (n.d) *Byron clinic Website quote from Marcia Linehan.*
Retrieved from https://byronclinic.com/marsha-linehan-radical-
acceptance/

MedlinePlus. (n.d.). *Why is it important to know my family health history?*
Retrieved from https://medlineplus.gov/genetics/understanding/
inheritance/familyhistory/

National Fatherhood Initiative. (2021). *The Proof is in: father absence
harms children.* Retrieved from https://www.fatherhood.org/father-
absence-statistic

National Institute of Mental health (n.d.). Looking at my genes: what can they
tell me about my mental health? Retrieved from
https://www.nimh.nih.gov/health/publications/looking-at-my-genes

National Institute of Mental Health. (n.d.).Help for mental illness. Retrieved
from https://www.nimh.nih.gov/health/find-help

Office of the Surgeon General (n.d.) *My family health portrait.* Retrieved from
https://phgkb.cdc.gov/FHH/html/index.html

Rosenberg, J. and Wilcox, B. (2006). *The importance of fathers in the healthy development of children.* Retrieved from https://www.childwelfare.gov/pubpdfs/fatherhood.pdf

Saakvitne, K., Gamble, S., Pearlman, L.A., Tabor, B. (2000). *Risking connection a training curriculum for working with survivors of childhood abuse.* Baltimore, MD: The Sidran Institute Press

Sokol, L., and Fox, M.G. (2019). *The comprehensive clinician's guide to cognitive behavioral therapy.* Eau Claire, WI: PESI Publishing & Media

Stosney, Steven, Ph.D. (2018). *The function of anger and resentment.* Retrieved from https://www.psychologytoday.com/us/blog/anger-in-the-age-entitlement/201812/the-function anger-and resentment

U.S. Census Bureau. (2020). *Living Arrangements of Children Under 18 Years Old: 1960 to present.* Washington, D.C.: U.S. Census Bureau

Wilmore, L., Mac B., Hutcherson, W., Tompkins S., Aronson, P., Borkow, M. (Executive Producers). (2001-2006). *The Bernie Mac Show.*

About the Author

Erika Daniels worked in the mental health field for over twenty-seven years and has been a Licensed Clinical Social Worker since 2003. She received her Bachelor of Arts degree in Sociology and her Master of Social Welfare degree from the University of California, Los Angeles. Erika has vast experience addressing mental health issues by utilizing evidence-based treatments and helping thousands of individuals throughout her career.

Erika currently practices as a clinical therapist in Southern California, and her diverse caseload includes adults and children with absent father issues. She also launched a Bring Dads Back Campaign to advocate for father involvement in children's lives.

Erika is a Christian, a wife, a mother, and a grandmother. When she is not helping others heal, she enjoys spending time with her family, playing the violin, songwriting, music producing, and doing ministry work at her church.

You can connect with me on:

https://www.reunitysolutions.com

https://www.facebook.com/reunitysolutions

https://www.facebook.com/bringdadsback

www.ingramcontent.com/pod-product-compliance
Lightning Source LLC
Chambersburg PA
CBHW070715130626
46553CB00005B/2001